LEE COUNTY LIBRARY
SANFORD, N. C.

Sporting Heritage

SPORTING HERITAGE

A Guide to Halls of Fame,
Special Collections and Museums in the
United States and Canada

Guy Lewis and Gerald Redmond

SOUTH BRUNSWICK AND NEW YORK: A. S. BARNES AND COMPANY
LONDON: THOMAS YOSELOFF LTD

© 1974 by A. S. Barnes and Co.

A. S. Barnes and Co., Inc.
Cranbury, New Jersey 08512

Thomas Yoseloff Ltd
108 New Bond Street
London W1Y OQX, England

Library of Congress Cataloging in Publication Data

Lewis, Guy.
    Sporting heritage; a guide to halls of fame, special collections, and museums in the United States and Canada.

    1. Sports museums—United States—Directories.   2. Sports museums—Canada—Directories.   I. Redmond, Gerald, 1934– joint author.   II. Title.
III. Title: Hall of fame.
GV583.L48   1974   796'.074'013   73-6391
ISBN 0-498-01306-5

PRINTED IN THE UNITED STATES OF AMERICA

CONTENTS

Acknowledgments	9
Introduction	13
PART I New England and New York State	
The Adirondack Museum	
Blue Mountain Lake, New York	19
The Gladding International Sport Fishing Museum	
South Otselic, New York	20
The National Museum of Racing	
Saratoga Springs, New York	21
The National Baseball Hall of Fame and Museum	
Cooperstown, New York	22
Hall of Fame of the Trotter	
Goshen, New York	24
Naismith Memorial Basketball Hall of Fame	
Springfield, Massachusetts	25
National Lawn Tennis Hall of Fame and Tennis Museum	
Newport, Rhode Island	26
PART II Middle Atlantic States and New York City	
"Golf House"	
Far Hills, New Jersey	53
National Art Museum of Sport	
New York, New York	54
The American Bicycle Hall of Fame	
Staten Island, New York	55
The C. Christopher Morris Cricket Library and Collection	
Haverford, Pennsylvania	56
PART III Southeastern States	
The Lacrosse Hall of Fame and Museum	
Baltimore, Maryland	65
National Jockeys Hall of Fame	
Baltimore, Maryland	66
The National Rifle Association Museum	
Washington, D. C.	67

James River Country Club's Golf Museum
    Newport News, Virginia   68
The Joe Weatherly Stock Car Museum
    Darlington, South Carolina   69
Museum of Speed
    Daytona Beach, Florida   70
Circus Hall of Fame
    Sarasota, Florida   71
Ringling Museum of the Circus
    Sarasota, Florida   72
The International Swimming Hall of Fame
    Fort Lauderdale, Florida   74

PART IV Middle Western States

St. Louis Sports Hall of Fame
    St. Louis, Missouri   91
Professional Football Hall of Fame
    Canton, Ohio   93
Woman's International Bowling Congress Hall of Fame
    Columbus, Ohio   94
The A.T.A. Hall of Fame and Trapshooting Museum
    Vandalia, Ohio   95
American Association of Collegiate Baseball Coaches Hall of Fame
    Kalamazoo, Michigan   96
The Air Museum of the Experimental Aircraft Association
    Franklin, Wisconsin   97
Circus World Museum
    Baraboo, Wisconsin   98
National Ski Hall of Fame
    Ishpeming, Michigan   100
United States Hockey Hall of Fame
    Eveleth, Minnesota   101
The Indianapolis Motor Speedway Museum
    Indianapolis, Indiana   102

PART V Southwestern States

National Cowboy Hall of Fame and Western Heritage Center
    Oklahoma City, Oklahoma   125
National Softball Hall of Fame
    Oklahoma City, Oklahoma   127
The Houston Baseball Museum
    Houston, Texas   128

PART VI Rocky Mountain and West Coast States

Western America Skisport Museum
    Auburn, California   135

San Jose State College Sports Library San Jose, California	136
United Savings-Helms Athletic Foundation and United Savings-Helms Hall Los Angeles, California	137
The Rose Bowl Hall of Fame Pasadena, California	140
San Diego Hall of Champions San Diego, California	141

PART VII Canada

The Canadian Golf Museum Quebec City, Quebec	153
The International Hockey Hall of Fame and Museum Kingston, Ontario	154
Canada's Sports Hall of Fame and Hockey Hall of Fame Toronto, Ontario	156
The K. A. Auty Memorial Library St. Catherines, Ontario	158
The National Ski Museum Ottawa, Ontario	159
The Canadian Football Hall of Fame Hamilton, Ontario	160
Daredevil Hall of Fame Niagara Falls, Ontario	162
Aquatic Hall of Fame and Museum of Canada, Inc. Winnipeg, Manitoba	164
Aquarium and Horseman's Hall of Fame Calgary, Alberta	166
The Edmonton Hall of Fame Edmonton, Alberta	168
The British Columbia Sports Hall of Fame Vancouver, British Columbia	169
The British Columbia Ski Hall of Fame Rossland, British Columbia	170

ACKNOWLEDGMENTS

The production of this guide would not have been possible without the generous assistance and cooperation of many people, particularly those associated with the halls of fame, museums, and other institutions that are included. The authors would like to express their gratitude to the following people who gave so willingly of their time to provide information and photographs:

Gaylord R. Aver, Executive Director, Avery F. Blake, President (1971), and Douglas C. Turnbull, Jr., President (1969), the Lacrosse Hall of Fame Foundation; W. A. Aylott, Librarian, K. A. Auty Memorial Cricket Library, Ridley College, St. Catherines, Ontario; Vaughan Lawson Baird, Aquatic Hall of Fame and Museum of Canada, Inc., Pan-Am Pool, Winnipeg; Al Bloemaker, Indianapolis Motor Speedway Museum, 4790 West 16th Street, Box 24152 Speedway, Indiana 46224; George Bowditch, Curator, and Mrs. Margaret Lamy, Public Relations, Adirondack Museum, Blue Mountain Lake, New York 12812; William Berry, Historian, for information in Ski Hall of Fame, Ishpeming, Michigan, and Western Skisport Museum, Auburn, California; M. Colwell, Manager, Rose Bowl Hall of Fame, Tournament House, 391 South Orange Grove Boulevard, Pasadena, California 91105; Howard Comfort, The C. Christopher Morris Cricket Library and Collection, Haverford College Library, Pennsylvania; Robert Culp, American Association of College Baseball Coaches Hall of Fame, Athletic Department, Western Michigan University, Kalamazoo, Michigan; Ward Cruickshank, II, Executive Director, National Art Museum of Sport, Madison Square Garden Center, New York City; William F. Dawson, Executive Director, International Swimming Hall of Fame, Fort Lauderdale, Florida; A. T. Emerson, Jr., Executive Director, Hall of Champions, Balboa Park, San Diego, California 92101; J. W. Fitsell, Curator and Secretary, The International Hockey Hall of Fame, Kingston, Ontario; (Mrs.) M. Fleck, Secretary, The British Columbia Sports Hall of Fame, B. C. Building Pacific National

Exhibition, Vancouver, B.C.; C. P. Fox, Director, Circus World Museum, Baraboo, Wisconsin; Ron Ferguson, City of Edmonton Parks and Recreation Department, Edmonton, Alberta, for information on the Edmonton Hall of Fame; Martha Fowler, for information on National Jockeys Hall of Fame, Pimlico Race Course, Baltimore, Maryland; Dr. William F. Gustafson, Department of Physical Education, San Jose State College, San Jose, California; H. Rae Grinnell, Chairman, and Miss M. E. Brough, National Ski Museum, 457A Sussex Drive, Ottawa, Ontario; Roland C. Geist, American Bicycle Hall of Fame, Richmondtown Restoration Museum, Staten Island, N.Y.; Roger A. Godwin, Executive Director, United States Hockey Hall of Fame, Eveleth, Minnesota; (Mrs.) R. M. Haire, Curator, National Lawn Tennis Hall of Fame and Tennis Museum, 194 Bellevue Avenue, Newport, Rhode Island; William B. Hall, former Director of Public Relations, and Dr. Bradley J. Kwenski, Executive Manager, Circus Hall of Fame, Sarasota, Florida 33578; Jacqueline J. Jordan, Director, St. Louis Sports Hall of Fame, Civic Center, Busch Memorial Stadium, 100 Stadium Plaza, St. Louis, Missouri 63102; J. R. Jones, Secretary, Canadian Football Hall of Fame Committee, Hamilton, Ontario; Norma Kirkendall, Manager, and Charles W. Westlake, Public Relations Manager, Woman's International Bowling Congress Hall of Fame, 1225 Dublin Road, Columbus, Ohio 43215; Floyd N. Lane, Director, Darlington Raceway, Darlington, South Carolina 29532; Mrs. Edith Long, Librarian, National Cowboy Hall of Fame, 1700 E. 63rd Street, Oklahoma City, Oklahoma 73111; Robert W. Lowe, Curator, National Rifle Association Museum, 1600 Rhode Island Avenue, Washington, D.C. 20036; Mrs. Elaine E. Mann, Director, National Museum of Racing, Saratoga Springs, New York 12866; J. D. McDonald, President, Rossland Historical Museum Association (British Columbia Ski Hall of Fame), P.O. Box 26, Rossland, B.C.; Hugh McKinley, Manager, Amateur Trapshooting Association, Headquarters, Vandalia, Ohio, U.S.A.; J. W. McKennon, Acting Curator, Mrs. Ann Johnson, Secretary, Publicity Department, and Mrs. Jean H. Houtchens, Information Department, Ringling Museum of the Circus, Sarasota, Florida; Paul H. Poberezny, President, Air Museum of the Experimental Aircraft Association, 11311 W. Forest Home Avenue, Franklin, Wisconsin; Philip A. Pines, Director, Hall of Fame of the Trotter, Goshen, New York 10924; Dr. Barry Pelton, University of Houston, Cullen Boulevard, Houston, Texas 77004; Donald E. Porter, Executive Secretary, Amateur Softball Association Hall of Fame, Park Avenue and Broadway, Oklahoma City, Oklahoma 73102; M. H. Reid, Curator, Canada's Sports Hall of Fame and Hockey Hall of Fame, Exhibition Park, Toronto

Acknowledgments

2B; David C. Rohrer, Gladding Corporation, P.O. Box 260, Syracuse, N.Y. 13201, for information on The Gladding International Sport Fishing Museum; W. Lyn Stewart, Hon. Secretary, The Canadian Golf Museum and Historical Institute, Kingsway Park, Mountain Road, Aylmer East, Quebec; W. R. Schroeder, Director, United Savings—Helms Hall, 9800 Sepulveda Boulevard, Los Angeles, California 90045; Ken Smith, Director, and Howard C. Talbot, Jr., Treasurer, National Baseball Hall of Fame and Museum, Cooperstown, New York 13326; Janet Seagle, Art Editor, Golf House, P.O. Box Golf, Far Hills, New Jersey; Donald R. Smith, Director of Public Relations, Pro Football's Hall of Fame, Canton, Ohio 44708; William R. Tuthill, Owner, Museum of Speed, P.O. Box 4170, Daytona Beach, Florida 32021; Lee Williams, Director, Naismith Memorial Basketball Hall of Fame, 460 Alden Street, Springfield, Massachusetts; Louis N. Wolfe, Director, Niagara Falls Museum, 1651 River Road, Niagara Falls, Ontario; K. N. Zurosky, Curator, Calgary Brewery Aquarium and Horseman's Hall of Fame, 1892 15th Street S.E., Calgary 22, Alberta.

The authors are also grateful for material received from the James River Country Club Golf Museum, near Newport News, Virginia.

INTRODUCTION

Rich sporting heritages belong to the people of Canada and the United States, and fortunately much thoughtful consideration has been given to the preservation of this aspect of the past. For, across both countries are located numerous institutions which house the documents and artifacts of bygone days in many sports. Whether the facility is called a museum or hall of fame matters little, as efforts in both instances are directed toward the preservation of records in the forms of manuscripts, books, documents, photographs, or memorabilia, and the presentation of visual displays relative to the history of the particular sport in ways that are informative and entertaining. Thus the institutions serve to satisfy the interest of students of the sporting past as well as those persons who find pleasure and profit in vicariously experiencing the great moments in the history of sport.

Guy Lewis
University of Massachusetts
Gerald Redmond
University of Alberta

Sporting Heritage

PART I
New England and New York State

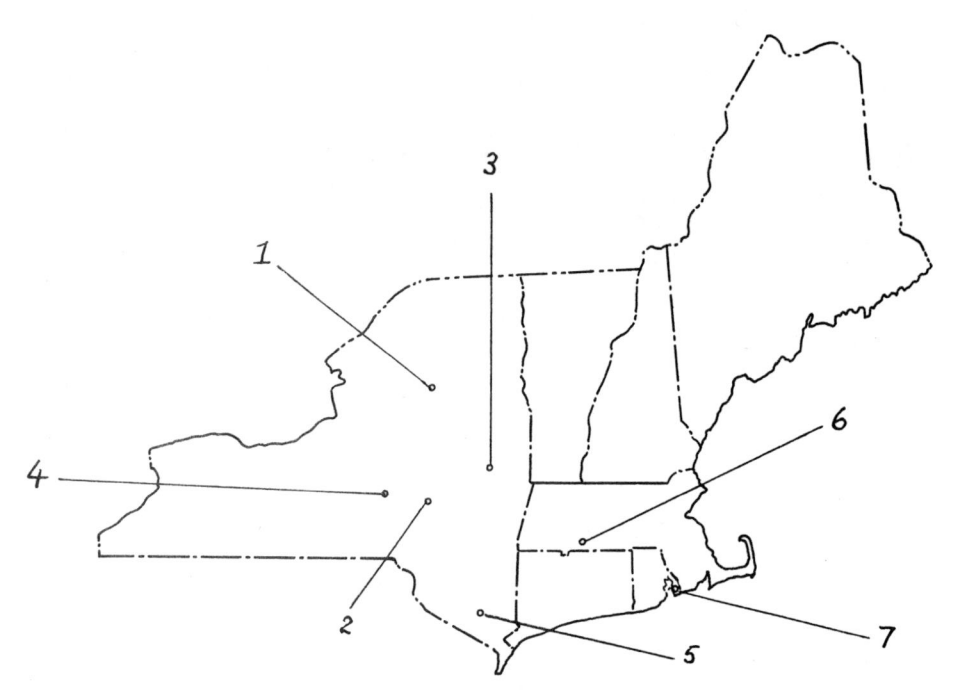

NEW ENGLAND AND NEW YORK STATE

1. Adirondack Museum
2. National Baseball Hall of Fame
3. National Museum of Racing
4. Gladding International Sport Fishing Museum
5. Hall of Fame of the Trotter
6. Naismith Memorial Basketball Hall of Fame
7. National Lawn Tennis Hall of Fame

THE ADIRONDACK MUSEUM
Blue Mountain Lake, New York

"Man's Relationship to the Adirondacks" is the theme of this indoor-outdoor history museum, located high on a shoulder of Blue Mountain, overlooking the lake and commanding magnificent views.

Dioramas, an electrically-activated relief map of the six-million acre Adirondack State Park, and changing exhibitions of paintings and prints provide a visual introduction to an area whose lakes, mountains, and forests have drawn visitors for a century and a half. Featured in its outstanding collection of small boats, extending from canoes to a lake steamer, is the Adirondack guide-boat, a light but sturdy craft developed specifically for use on the region's miles of interconnecting waterways.

More than 50 horse-drawn vehicles are arranged in exhibits showing the patterns of change during the nineteenth-century from farming, lumbering, and mining to the resort business; also included is the private Pullman car once owned by August Belmont.

Hunting rifles, stoves, an Adirondack camp, a hermit's cabin, a small aquarium, equipment used in logging, icing and maple sugaring, and the locomotive and two cars from one of the shortest standard-gauge railroad lines known also are shown, along with more than 300 photographs of early scenes.

A privately supported, nonprofit, educational institution chartered by the State of New York in 1954, the museum opened to the public in 1957. In 1970 it received the Award of Merit of the American Association of State and Local History and, in 1969, the annual award of the New York State Council on the Arts.

DATES: Open June 15 through October 15
HOURS: 10 A.M. to 5 P.M. every day including Sundays
ADMISSION: Adults $2.00, Children $.50
Reduced rates for organized groups

THE GLADDING INTERNATIONAL SPORT FISHING MUSEUM

South Otselic, New York

This first sport fishing museum was sponsored by the 156-year-old Gladding Corporation, the oldest manufacturer of sporting goods continuously in business since its 1816 Chenango County founding. The museum was opened on September 16, 1972, and was chartered as a nonprofit institution to restore and preserve relics of recreational and sport fishing, and to promote the need for greater conservation efforts. The museum building is a 142-year-old eight-sided mansion that has long been a landmark in the hamlet of South Otselic.

Three floors of exhibits are available to visitors. Original watercolors of New York State fish, loaned by the State Environmental Conservation Department, line the walls of the reception area. Some of the works by the late Maynard Reece, the famous wildlife artist, can also be viewed at the Museum, as well as early steel engravings of noted fishing scenes. In the Salt Water Room are mounted fish and deep-sea rods, including Lou Marron's huge rod with which he caught the world's largest (1182 lbs.) broadbill swordfish. Many early and interesting tackle and equipment exhibits feature creels, tailer and landing nets, and various fishing rods. The world's two smallest reels can be seen next to a gigantic French reel, believed to be the world's largest. One of the hundreds of lures displayed is an ancient polished stone and handcrafted trolling rig used by Greenland Eskimos.

The museum library contains rare editions of famous fishing books, such as an 1875 edition of Dame Juliana Berners's *Fysshe and Fysshynge* (1496 A.D.), and three copies of Izaak Walton's *The Compleat Angler*. Gerald Mayer, Gladding Corporation president and chairman of the museum Board of Trustees, has expressed the intention to continually add to this new facility, and for years to come enthusiasts will obtain benefit and pleasure by visiting the unique Gladding International Sport Fishing Museum.

DATES: May 1 to October 1 (1973)
HOURS: 1 P.M. to 5 P.M. weekdays
10 A.M. to 5 P.M. Saturdays and Sundays
ADMISSION: FREE

New England and New York State

THE NATIONAL MUSEUM OF RACING

Saratoga Springs, New York

The National Museum of Racing was founded in 1950 and was granted a charter by the State of New York that same year. Exhibits were located in temporary quarters until the present building was completed in 1955. Located across the street from the famous Saratoga Race Course (America's oldest operating Thoroughbred track), the building houses the museum and hall of fame.

The handsome Georgian-Colonial design brick structure contains one of the world's greatest collections of equine art, trophies, sculptures, and memorabilia of the "sport of kings" from its earliest days. There are approximately 250 oil paintings on exhibition, of such famous race horses as Man O'War and Lexington, as well as portraits of famous racing personages. There are also 200 sets of famous racing colors including those of George D. Widener, Bing Crosby, Sir Winston Churchill, and Queen Elizabeth II. Trophies won by famous horses are on display. Immortals of the sport—trainers, jockeys, and horses—are enshrined here in the hall of fame, which is located in the rear of the imposing edifice. Special exhibits and films relating to the sport are shown daily during the racing season (August). There is also a small souvenir and gift department.

DATES: Year Round
HOURS: 10 A.M. to 5 P.M. weekdays
12 noon to 5 P.M. Saturday
Open Sunday: from June 15 to September 30, 12 noon to 5 P.M.
During racing season: 9:30 A.M. to 8 P.M. daily
ADMISSION: FREE

THE NATIONAL BASEBALL HALL OF FAME AND MUSEUM

Cooperstown, New York

The idea for a national baseball museum came from Stephen C. Clark, a native of Cooperstown, New York. Clark interested Alexander Cleland in the project and Cleland successfully solicited the assistance of the leading figures in baseball. One, Ford C. Frick, then president of the National League, suggested the plans be expanded to include a shrine to former great players. In 1939 the National Baseball Hall of Fame and Museum opened; the National Baseball Library was dedicated in the summer of 1968.

In this three-story structure of brick and stone, situated in a village typical of those in which the national game was first played, are the treasured mementos from more than a century of baseball. The hall of fame occupies a separate wing of the museum, directly to the rear of the entrance room, and is a room 85 feet long, 43 feet wide, and 25 feet high, with pillars of fine Vermont marble supporting the lofty ceiling. Professional baseball's greatest honor is the attainment of a plaque here, a feat that only a few of the thousands of players have accomplished.

Hall of fame members are honored by exhibits particularly on the main floor where lockers, uniforms, bats, balls, and gloves of the stars are on view. All World Series winners are seen in the second-floor gallery where the Temple Cup is shown, emblematic of championship in the previous century. Current most-valuable players and all-stars are on this flight where the new Negro League photographic collection is located. The Babe Ruth wing, and views of old stars, are on the third floor. The achievement room is in the basement where no-hitters, perfect games, record long games, up-to-date Rawlings Gold and Silver Glove awards, the Ebbets Field cornerstone and lockers, equipment, and, everywhere, paintings and trophies of old favorites are located.

The gray-stoned library building, on the lawn behind the main hall of fame, is dedicated to writing, photography, art, and broadcasting. The resident historian and librarian presents a file on every major-league player since 1871, as well as thousands of pictures and documents. Motion picture programs of famous old stars and modern players are run daily in the library basement projection room during the summer. The upstairs library stalls are open to researchers.

DATES: Open 7 days a week and all holidays except Thanksgiving, Christmas, and New Year's Day.
HOURS: Summer—May 1 to October 31, 9 A.M. to 9 P.M.
Winter—November 1 to April 30, 9 A.M. to 9 P.M.
ADMISSION: Adults $1.50
Children (7 years to 15 years) $.40

HALL OF FAME OF THE TROTTER
Goshen, New York

The rear doors of this attractive building open on to Historic Track, a National Registered Historic Landmark. It is the only sporting site in the nation to have received this designation. One of the many feature attractions is the viewing of the horses in action during the spring, summer, or autumn. The museum preserves the memorabilia of the sport of harness racing, and immortalizes the great men and horses of the sport. Originally a stable, the Hall of Fame of the Trotter "uses its stalls as exhibition rooms, its haychutes as miniature stages, its loft to display sulkies as well as the original Phillips mobile starting gate." Films about trotting and pacing horse history are shown, and the museum is full of interesting exhibits and dioramas. Over 30,000 people visited in 1969, but the museum does a lot of "visiting," too. It is particularly active in circulating its exhibits to other galleries, libraries, schools, universities, museums, and civic institutions.

DATES: All year
HOURS: 10 A.M. to 5 P.M. daily
Sundays and holidays 1:30 P.M. to 5 P.M.
ADMISSION: FREE

NAISMITH MEMORIAL BASKETBALL HALL OF FAME

Springfield, Massachusetts

The national hall of fame for the youngest major sport is situated on the Springfield College campus at 460 Alden Street, on a site personally selected by Dr. Naismith, and designated by the coaches, players, and administrators of basketball—amateur, interscholastic, intercollegiate, and professional. The large building covers more than 23,000 square feet of area at a cost of approximately $650,000.

Inside is the Hillyard Lobby, containing the souvenir area, a section devoted to the game's founder, Dr. James Naismith, and a special display on the participation of the Hillyard Chemical Company in basketball. Adjoining the lobby is the picturesque Hall of Founders, listing the various contributions to the hall of fame. The Honors Court has cathedral-like ceiling-to-floor plaques that are individually hand painted for those elected to distinction. Among those persons honored as game's great heroes are players, coaches, referees, and contributors. Four great teams are enshrined—The First Team, the Original Celtics, the Buffalo Y.M.C.A. "Germans," and the Original Renaissance, while 76 individuals are enshrined through 1971. There is also a replica of the original floor of the Armory Y.M.C.A., with the peach basket first used, a chronological history of the game, and many other artifacts from 1891 to the present. The second floor is devoted to area displays of all organizations associated with the game. On display are the Naismith Cup and the Raposo Cup (emblematic of men's and women's international championships), the NBA Section, NCAA Section, NABC Section, and the Hickox Library is available to researchers and browsers. The lower level also has the Converse Room, used for hourly movies, more displays, and a refreshment area.

DATES: Open all year round. Closed Christmas, New Year's, and Thanksgiving
HOURS: 10 A.M. to 5 P.M. daily
1 P.M. to 5 P.M. Sunday
ADMISSION: $1.25 Adults
$.75 Students, 14 through college
$.50 Students, under 14
Groups of 10 or more: $.50 students; $1.00 adults

NATIONAL LAWN TENNIS HALL OF FAME AND TENNIS MUSEUM

Newport, Rhode Island

The United States Lawn Tennis Association gave official permission for the establishment of the National Lawn Tennis Hall of Fame following the proposal by James H. Van Alen in 1952 that one be established at the Newport Casino. Dedication ceremonies were held in the summer of 1955. Selection of the casino as the location of the hall was appropriate, as it was the site of the first U.S. Lawn Tennis Association Championships in 1881.

The museum has four large rooms, each about 40 feet long, filled with photographs, rackets, paintings, statuary, and silver trophies. It has antique rackets and other historic tennis equipment, as well as a model tennis court, and a good collection of tennis books. There is also a little theater, used as an auditorium for tennis movies. A group of distinguished tennis personalities is enshrined in the Tennis Hall of Fame, which also has a tennis court opposite the entrance. Tennis may sometimes be played by visitors on the casino grass courts, if arrangements are made in advance. Plans for future development call for the construction of an indoor tennis court and a gift shop. A display featuring tennis costumes of former times is also under consideration by the staff.

DATES: May 15 to October 27
HOURS: 9:30 A.M. to 5 P.M. weekdays
11 A.M. to 5 P.M. Sundays and holidays
ADMISSION: Adults $.50 and children $.25

The Adirondack Museum

The First Snow—Deer-Shooting on the Shatagee, 1855, by Arthur Fitzwilliam Tait (1819—1905). (Courtesy Adirondack Museum)

The Indians who trapped and hunted in the Adirondacks took advantage of its vast system of interconnecting waterways, just as did the white men who followed them. Although only a reproduction of the Indian craft, this fine birch bark canoe on exhibit at the Adirondack Museum makes those earliest visitors seem awfully real for this youngster! Beside it is a dugout recovered from the bottom of an Adirondack lake. (Courtesy Adirondack Museum)

Blue Mountain Lake itself is an important exhibit at the Adirondack Museum, too. Visitors stroll through a combination of indoor and outdoor exhibits located on a 30-acre site that was formerly a resort hotel, lying about a mile from the village of Blue Mountain Lake. The design of the campus retains the charm of the setting, with its spectacular view. (Courtesy Adirondack Museum)

Early power boats are exhibited in the outdoor pond. In the background are the passenger steamer *Osprey* and the private launch *Whileaway* formerly owned by the Whitney family. The relatively recent electric-powered fishing boat, foreground, contrasts with the *Skeeter*, right rear, which was one of the first speedboats to operate on an Adirondack lake. The two-ton outfit, powered by a huge, six-cylinder gasoline engine, could reach 25 miles an hour, an unheard of speed when it was launched in 1906 on Raquette Lake. (Courtesy Adirondack Museum)

The writer George Washington Sears, known as "Nessmuk," traveled for miles through the Adirondack wilderness in his tiny, 10½-pound canoe, *Sairy Gamp*, center, specially built by the famed boat craftsman, J. Henry Rushton. It is on permanent loan to the Adirondack Museum from the Smithsonian Institution. The museum's collection of small boats is rated among the best in the country. (Courtesy Adirondack Museum)

The display of small boats at the Adirondack Museum is among the best in the country. Here in the Callahan Memorial Boat Building, as well as outdoors, they are shown in their natural element. The museum has an especially fine collection of the famed Adirondack guide-boat. (Courtesy Adirondack Museum)

Water Witch, a racing sloop formerly owned and sailed by Ogden Reid, was one of a single-design class built specially for the families who made their summer homes on the St. Regis lakes. It now floats in its own pond inside this plastic bubble, visible from the highway adjacent to the Adirondack Museum. The museum's collection of small boats has been called by leading experts one of the finest in the country. (Courtesy Adirondack Museum)

These two visitors enjoy a nostalgic moment, recalling some trips of their own with a guide boat that was designed to be used on the interconnecting system of lakes and streams in the region. The boat was light enough to be carried by one man on the portages, or "carries," as they are known in the Adirondacks. (Courtesy Adirondack Museum)

New England and New York State

The Gladding International Sport Fishing Museum, South Otselic, N.Y.

1770 "Multiplier." (Courtesy The Gladding International Sport Fishing Museum)

The world's largest spinning reel. (Courtesy The Gladding International Sport Fishing Museum)

New England and New York State

Golden Trout by Maynard Reece. (Courtesy The Gladding International Sport Fishing Museum)

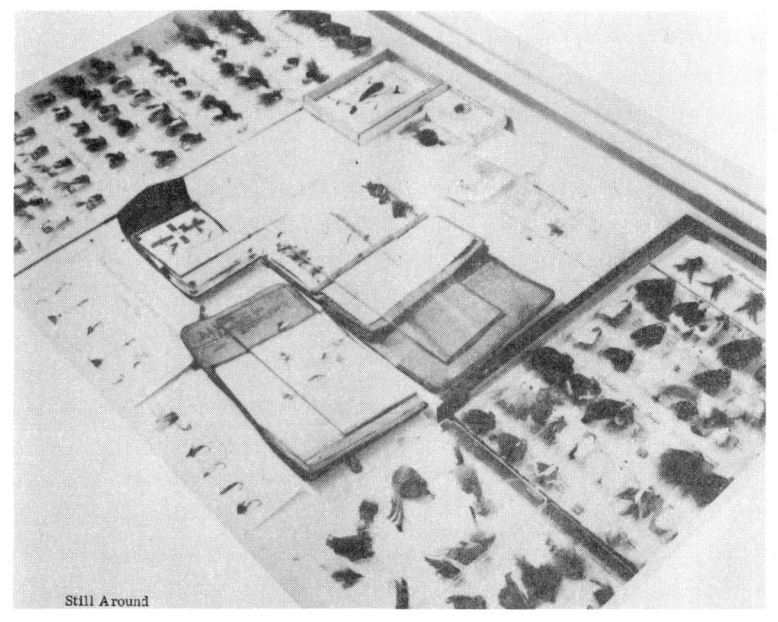

Still around. (Courtesy The Gladding International Sport Fishing Museum)

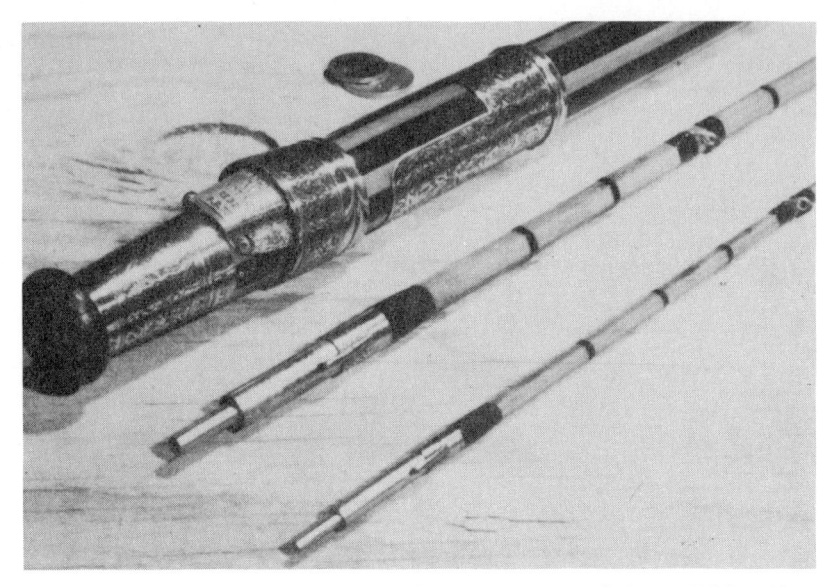

Hardy 1884 Special. (Courtesy The Gladding International Sport Fishing Museum)

Fit for a princess. (Courtesy The Gladding International Sport Fishing Museum)

New England and New York State

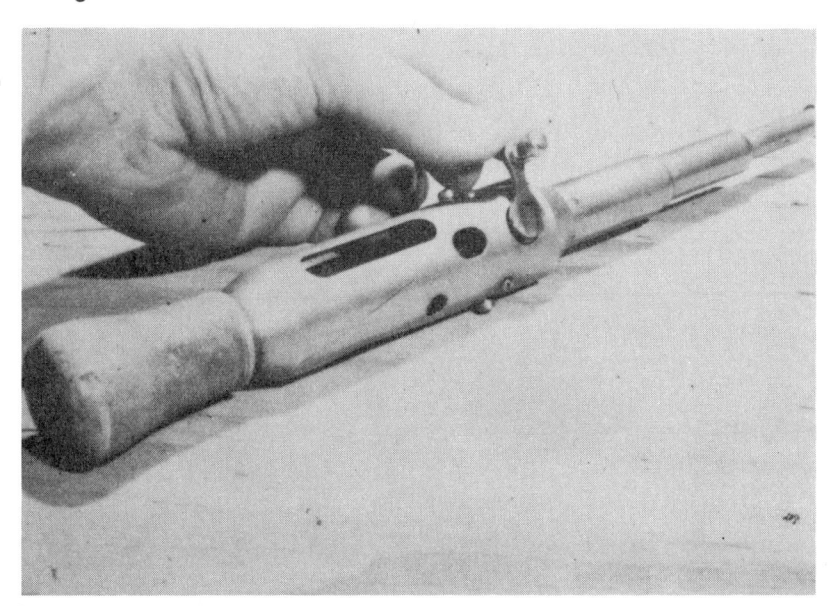

Early spin cast reel attempt. (Courtesy The Gladding International Sport Fishing Museum)

1880 Malloch. (Courtesy The Gladding International Sport Fishing Museum)

The National Museum of Racing. (Courtesy National Museum of Racing)

Lexington by Edward Troye. (Courtesy National Museum of Racing)

The First Futurity by L. Maurer, 1889. (Courtesy National Museum of Racing)

Oklahoma (Training Track) by Elmore Brown, 1954. (Courtesy National Museum of Racing)

Nashua (at Saratoga) by W. Smithson Broadhead, 1955. (Courtesy National Museum of Racing)

Man O' War (as a 2 yr. old) by F. B. Voss, 1919. (Courtesy National Museum of Racing)

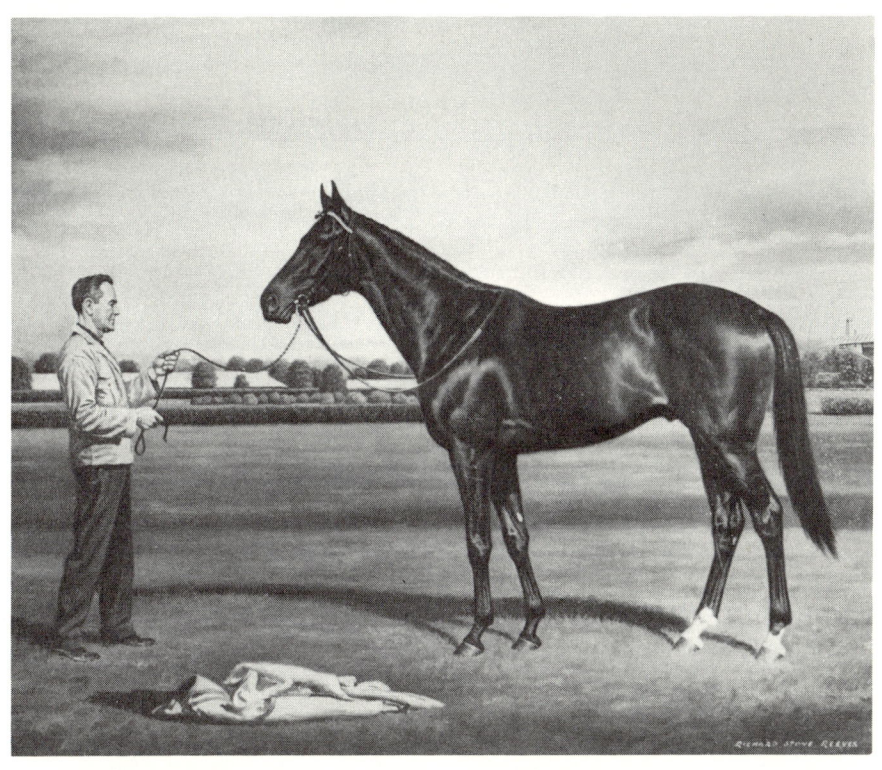

Kelso by Richard Stone Reeves. (Courtesy National Museum of Racing)

National Baseball Hall of Fame and Museum. (Courtesy National Baseball Hall of Fame)

National Baseball Library. (Courtesy National Baseball Library)

Statue made by Cincinnati fans in 1969, the year of baseball's centennial celebration. (Courtesy National Baseball Hall of Fame)

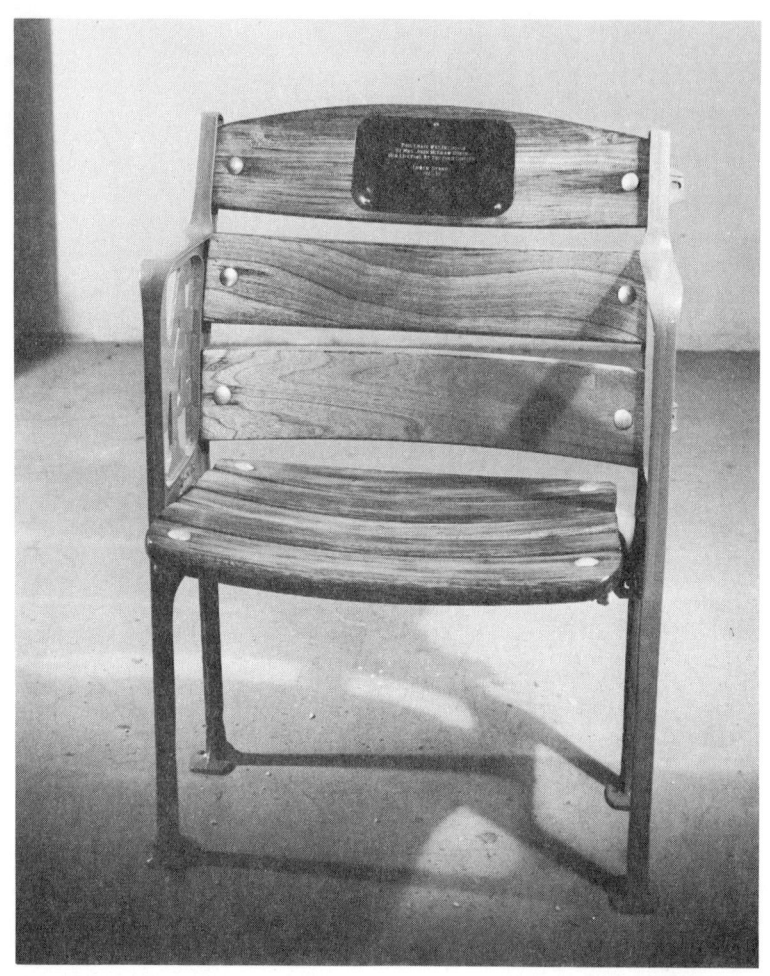

Chair from polo grounds occupied almost daily by Mrs. John McGraw, wife of the famous manager of the New York Giants. (Courtesy National Baseball Hall of Fame)

Ebbets Field cornerstone being examined by Sid C. Keener, Hall of Fame Director. (Courtesy National Baseball Hall of Fame)

The Temple Cup, world championship trophy in the 1890s. (Courtesy National Baseball Library)

An old poster display, located on the third floor of the main building. (Courtesy National Baseball Hall of Fame)

Hall of Fame of the Trotter. (Courtesy Hall of Fame of the Trotter)

Display at the Hall of Fame of the Trotter. (Courtesy Hall of Fame of the Trotter)

School children during a visit to the Hall of Fame of the Trotter. (Courtesy Hall of Fame of the Trotter)

Display at the Hall of Fame of the Trotter. (Courtesy Hall of Fame of the Trotter)

Naismith Memorial Basketball Hall of Fame. (Courtesy Naismith Memorial Basketball Hall of Fame)

New England and New York State

The Honors Court. (Courtesy Naismith Memorial Basketball Hall of Fame)

PART II
Middle Atlantic States and New York City

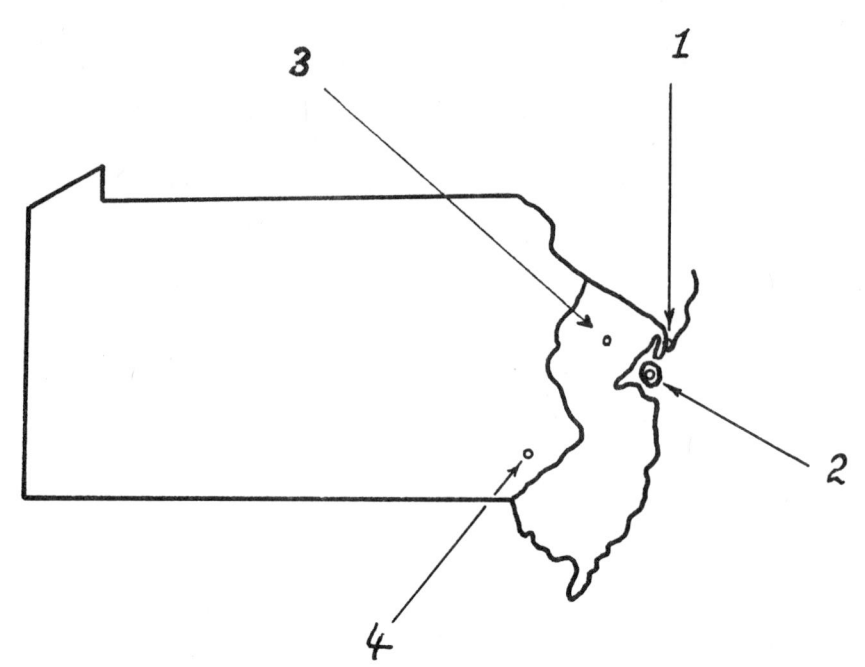

MIDDLE ATLANTIC STATES AND NEW YORK CITY

1. National Art Museum of Sport
2. American Bicycle Hall of Fame
3. U.S.G.A. Golf House
4. C. Christopher Morris Cricket Library and Collection

"GOLF HOUSE"

Route 512, P.O. Box Golf, Far Hills, New Jersey

The United States Golf Association, formed on December 22, 1894, has collected materials for a reference library and exhibits.

This golf museum and library is situated at the headquarters of the association in Far Hills, New Jersey. It has permanent exhibits of historical value, including famous clubs used in winning championships, such as Robert T. Jones, Jr.'s famous putter "Calamity Jane II." There is a fine collection of other clubs, balls, medals, pictures, portraits, and documents. One can see a statue and portrait of Ben Hogan, a head sculpture of Arnold Palmer, and a collection of medals won by Bobby Jones. The excellent golf library is available for reference.

DATES: Monday through Friday
HOURS: 9 A.M. to 5 P.M.
ADMISSION: FREE

NATIONAL ART MUSEUM OF SPORT

New York City

The National Art Museum of Sport was chartered in 1959 by the Board of Regents of the University of the State of New York as a nonprofit educational institution. Stimulated and guided by Founder-President Germain G. Glidden, the museum's collection expanded rapidly during the first decade. The 5000-square foot Gallery of Art is located in the Madison Square Garden Center.

The museum's aim is "to encourage a greater understanding of the fine arts and the competence they demand by enlisting on the side of art the public's intimate knowledge of and enthusiasm for sport." The museum's growing collection of paintings, sculpture, and drawings represents contemporary artists. It also sends exhibits to other parts of the United States and the world on appropriate occasions.

DATES: Year round
HOURS: 9:30 A.M. to 5:30 P.M. daily
ADMISSION: Adults $.50
Children under 14 $.25

THE AMERICAN BICYCLE HALL OF FAME

Staten Island

The idea for the American Bicycle Hall of Fame originated with officials of the Century Road Club Association of New York in 1958. During the next few years, funds and items for the collections were solicited and plans made for the establishment of a permanent home. Dedication Day ceremonies were held on June 2, 1968.

Although housed temporarily in the museum alcove, the American Bicycle Hall of Fame has had a $50,000 plot of land offered by President Loring McMillen of the Staten Island Historical Society, and plans a building of its own as soon as funds become available. Included in the present exhibits is the late Sykvain Segal's Syls Racing Columbia of 1900, and his century badges and medals, and the old Tribune racer on which James Paul made his New York-Atlantic City record in the 1920s. Famous people connected with the sport in the past, such as "Mile-a-Minute Murphy" and Thomas Stevens, who rode around the world in the nineteenth century on a high-wheel Columbia bicycle, have been elected to the American Bicycle Hall of Fame. Public support of this present hall will help to make the proposed new and larger hall of fame become a reality.

HOURS: 2 P.M. to 5 P.M. on Saturdays, Sundays, and holidays
ADMISSION: FREE

THE C. CHRISTOPHER MORRIS CRICKET LIBRARY AND COLLECTION

Haverford College, Haverford, Pennsylvania

The C. Christopher Morris Cricket Library and Collection is housed in a special exhibition room at the Magill Library of Haverford College, Haverford, Pennsylvania. It was officially opened in March 1969, after one of America's most distinguished cricketers, Dr. John A. Lester, had proposed in 1964 that a "cricket alcove" be planned in the expanded College Library. Mr. Morris and others acted upon the suggestion and the present facility, designed by Harbison, Hough, Livingston, and Larson, is the result. During its formative stages the enterprise was administered by a committee composed chiefly of Haverford College cricketers, but subsequently the management passed to a more inclusive C. C. Morris Cricket Library Association formed in 1970.

A nucleus of cricket literature already existed in the college library, but this has now been greatly increased from many other sources, especially by the donation of Mr. Morris's own cricket library. Outstanding items include a complete set of Wisden's *Cricketers Almanack* (1864 to date), two complete sets of the *American Cricketer* (1877–1929), and a copy of Sir Jeremiah Colman's *Noble Game of Cricket* presented by the Marylebone Cricket Club of London. As cataloguing proceeds, numerous other interesting and valuable books and pamphlets are becoming apparent. It is the association's intent to make the collection as complete a record as possible of the story of cricket in the United States and Canada. As it has often been referred to as "America's nursery of cricket," it is not surprising that the Philadelphia area is the best documented, but the larger intention is the ultimate goal. In addition, the collection includes considerable incidental material from other parts of the world.

The C. Christopher Morris Cricket Library and Collection also includes memorabilia of numerous cricketers. For example: the scrap books kept by Philadelphia cricketers on the various tours of England in the late nineteenth and early twenties centuries, trophies presented to Dr. Lester and the great bowler, J. Barton King, by Prince Ranjitsinhji, a bat presented by the famous Dr. W. G. Grace to G. D. Jessop and by him to the Merion Cricket Club in 1897, after he had made 1541 runs with it in only 9 innings, the bat with which Mr. Morris himself at the age of 20 made 164 runs against Nottingham at Trent Bridge, and a number of blazers and club ties, including a blazer from the Shanghai (China) Cricket Club, that formerly belonged to Dr. Harold E. Morris and that must be unique, a holograph letter from Dr. Grace to Dr. Lester, a letter from the Caldera (Chile) Cricket Club dated 1876 and illustrated with a charming watercolor, petit point belts such as young ladies of the last century made for their favorite cricketers, and autographed cricket balls, paintings, cups, and other trophies. Within its scope, the Morris Library is unique in North America and, with the exception of the museum at Lord's Cricket Ground in London, perhaps in the world.

It is open to the public by application to the circulation desk of the Haverford College Library at any time when the latter is open. At present the administrative secretary is in the room on Monday, Wednesday, and Friday afternoons, 1:30 P.M. to 4:30 P.M. Access for casual visitors or research purposes is also available by contacting either the president (1972) of the association, Howard Comfort, or Curator E. Rotan Sargent, both of whom are listed in the Philadelphia Eastern Main Line suburban telephone directory.

Ben Hogan, painted by J. Anthony Wills. (Courtesy Golf House)

Middle Atlantic States and New York City

Golf medals won by Bobby Jones. (Courtesy Golf House)

The Golf House, Far Hills, New Jersey. (Courtesy Golf House)

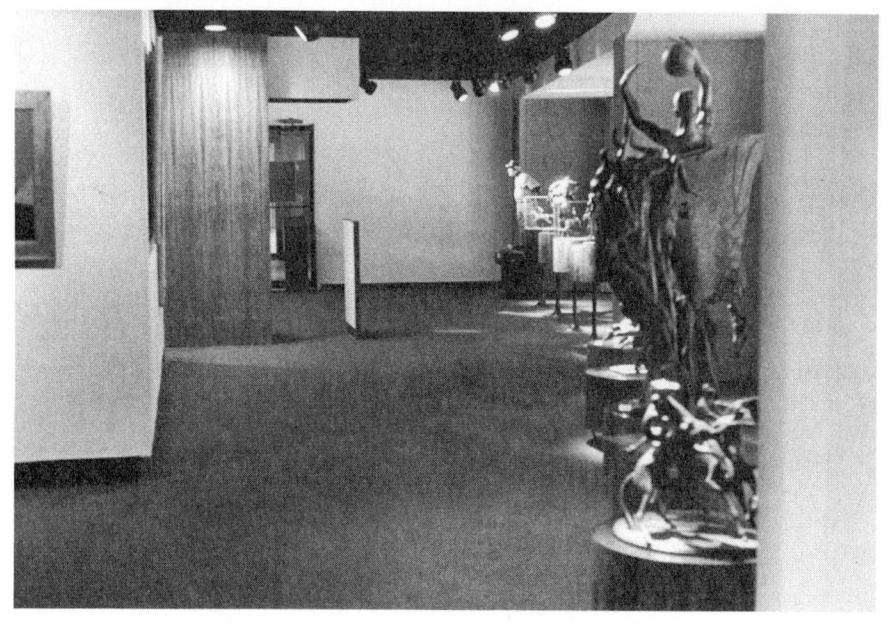

The National Art Museum of Sport. (Courtesy National Art Museum of Sport)

American Bicycle Hall of Fame. (Courtesy Al Hatos)

Interior of the C. Morris Cricket Library and Collection. (Courtesy Haverford College)

Interior of the C. Morris Cricket Library and Collection. (Courtesy Haverford College)

PART III
Southeastern States

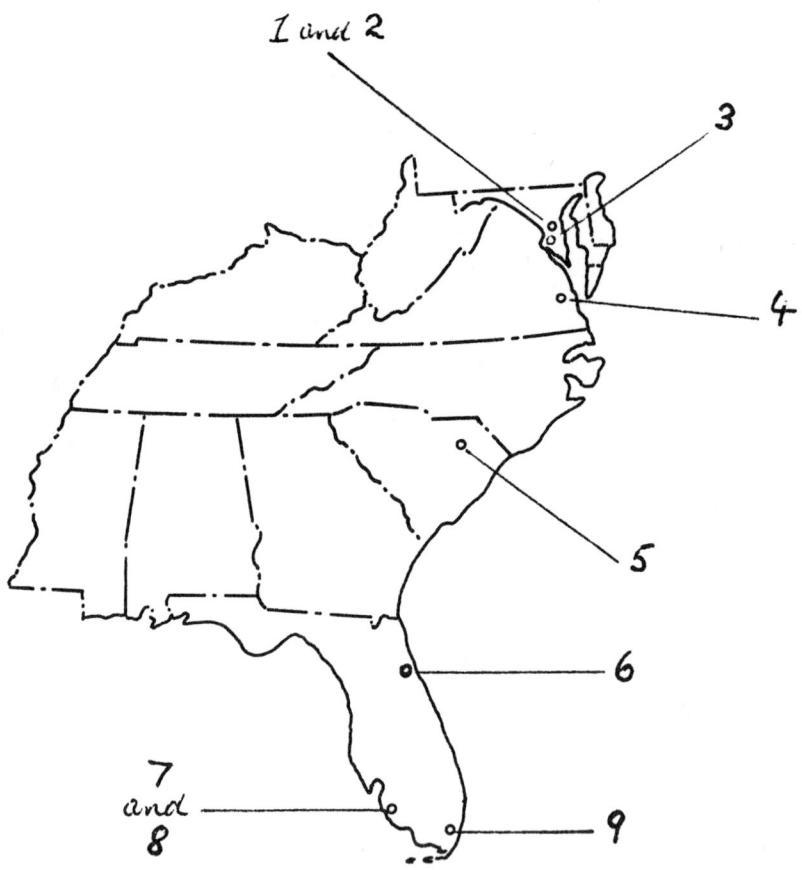

SOUTHEASTERN STATES

1. Lacrosse Hall of Fame
2. National Jockeys Hall of Fame
3. National Rifle Association Museum
4. James River Country Club Golf Museum
5. Joe Weatherly Stock Car Museum
6. Museum of Speed
7. Circus Hall of Fame
8. Ringling Museum of the Circus
9. International Swimming Hall of Fame

THE LACROSSE HALL OF FAME AND MUSEUM

Baltimore, Maryland

A movement to establish a Lacrosse Hall of Fame began in 1954, when the USILA set up a committee to investigate the matter. From the original concept of a Lacrosse Hall of Fame, the idea grew, and in 1959 the Lacrosse Hall of Fame Foundation, Inc., a Maryland Corporation, was chartered. It was felt that through its own charitable foundation, lacrosse could not only create its own hall of fame, but along with it a museum and a research library. It could also secure monies to assist in the promotion of lacrosse and program a clearing house for all problems connected with lacrosse.

Although much preliminary work was accomplished from 1959 to 1966, actual physical facilities did not come into being for the hall of fame and museum until June 10, 1966, when dedication ceremonies were held at Homewood. However, during the early stages, the officers and executive secretary had started the building of an endowment fund, set up both an alphabetical index and a geographical index of former lacrosse players, numbering 10,000, begun collecting the memorabilia of the game, and begun the promotion of the game in every way feasible with the limited funds and personnel available.

Today, at Homewood, utilizing 1200 square feet of space, lacrosse has a permanent home for all kinds of display and reference materials pertaining to the game, including pictures, lithographs, paintings, plaques, and busts of lacrosse "greats." Memorabilia of the game are imposingly displayed in cabinets. There is a library collection of pertinent books, magazine articles, a file of lacrosse guides, and miscellaneous documents of historical interest.

DATES: Mid-September to early June
HOURS: 9 A.M. to 5 P.M.
ADMISSION: FREE

NATIONAL JOCKEYS HALL OF FAME

Maryland

The National Jockeys Hall of Fame was founded in 1955 by officers of the Maryland Jockey Club. The gallery was destroyed by fire in 1966, but a new one has been put together and is located in the members' clubhouse at the Pimlico Race Course.

THE NATIONAL RIFLE ASSOCIATION MUSEUM

Washington, D.C. 20036

The National Rifle Association is a nonprofit organization, founded in 1871, with over a million current members. The NRA Museum originated about 36 years ago when a small collection of antique arms was displayed at the previous NRA headquarters in the Barr Building. When the association moved to 1600 Rhode Island Avenue, this collection was exhibited in a small room off the lobby, until it had to be placed in storage. The room was needed for working space due to the tremendous growth of the NRA following World War II. Fortunately, when the new Headquarters Building was opened in 1957, a new museum was established on the fourth floor, later moved to the first floor with 7,000 sq. ft. available for display.

At present there are over 1000 arms on display. The emphasis is upon the quality of the 72 exhibits contained in display cases that are numbered consecutively. Numbers 7 through 38 are on the first floor, and numbers 39 through 72 are on the second floor where there are several additional special displays. The evolutionary development of firearms from many countries is very well depicted, including many sporting guns and rifles for the shooting enthusiast. Visitors are also welcome to use the facilities of the Reading Room.

DATES: Open daily. The museum is closed on Christmas Day, New Year's Day, and Easter Sunday.
HOURS: 10 A.M. to 4 P.M.
ADMISSION: FREE

JAMES RIVER COUNTRY CLUB'S GOLF MUSEUM

Newport News, Virginia

The Golf Museum at the James River Country Club, Newport News, Virginia, was founded in 1932. It was made possible by financial support received from Archer M. Huntington. This museum has "the finest collection of antique golfing implements in this country or perhaps in the world"; this includes baffies, brassies, cleeks, jiggers, niblicks, and spoons. Altogether there are approximately 300 old clubs in the exhibition cases, headed by an old wooden putter from the year 1765 made by Simon Cossen of Leith, Scotland. The oldest iron club is a sand iron with a concave face of the period of 1820. A number of early American golf clubs are also on display. There are many exhibits from A. G. Spalding and Company. The history of the golf ball is very well depicted from the early feather balls down to the present day. One of the most attractive exhibits is a 12' x 5' scale model of the old course at St. Andrews, Scotland. One can also see artifacts of the old clubmakers' art, cups, medals, and trophies. There is an excellent collection of well-known golfing pictures. The museum's library of over 750 volumes is one of the largest collections of golf books in America.

DATES: Daily throughout the year, except Mondays
HOURS: Day and evening
ADMISSION: FREE

THE JOE WEATHERLY STOCK CAR MUSEUM

Darlington Raceway, Darlington, South Carolina

The Joe Weatherly Stock Car Museum opened in 1965 and since that time more than three million visitors have viewed the tributes to men and machines housed in this handsome facility. A project of the Board of Directors of the Darlington Raceway, the museum is named in honor of the popular and successful race driver, "Little Joe" Weatherly.

On exhibit are such automobiles as the first entry in the Southern 500, a 1950 Oldsmobile, Herb Thomas' famous Hudson Hornet, the Plymouth in which Johnny Mantz won the first Southern 500, the pink and white Ford used by Curtis Turner on the convertible circuit, the lavender Ford driven by the late Glenn ("Fireball") Roberts, and many others.

Then, too, visitors are privileged to view the trophies and memorabilia belonging to such outstanding stock car drivers as Weatherly, Roberts, "Buck" Baker, and Turner. Collections are arranged so that each special display is a chronicle of the career of a single driver. Finally, in addition to the trophies, photographs, automobiles and engines, special displays and other memorabilia, the building also contains The Southern Motorsports Press Association Hall of Fame. Here, recorded for present and future generations, are the names of the sports' outstanding performers of the past. At the time of the impressive annual ceremonies, enshrinement is bestowed upon other drivers.

HOURS: 9 A.M. to 12 noon, 2 P.M. to 5 P.M. daily
ADMISSION: FREE

MUSEUM OF SPEED
Daytona Beach, Florida 32021

Here in this showcase are famous boats, cars, and motorcycles that have all obtained world speed records. Visitors can view the incredible Bluebird in which Sir Malcolm Campbell recorded a speed of 330 m.p.h. at Daytona Beach in 1935. The Bluebird is 30 feet long, weighs 5 tons, and is powered by a special 2500 horsepower Rolls-Royce supercharged V12 engine. This engine alone cost the British government more than $75,000. Also featured in this unique collection is the 20-ft. long Green Monster, built in Akron, Ohio, by Art and Walter Arfons, and the first car to achieve 150 m.p.h. in a quarter mile from a standing start, and Don Garlits' World Championship Dragster that was the first to officially achieve 200 m.p.h. in a quarter mile.

Many champion American and foreign motorcycles on display span a period of over 60 years, as well as famous speedboats such as Miss America VIII, twice winner of the Harmsworth Trophy, and world record holder and cup winner, Tempo VI. Among stock car exhibits is the special "Smokey" Yunick-prepared Pontiac with which the great "Fireball" Roberts established his amazing records during the 1962 season at the Daytona International Speedway. The museum houses just about every type of racing engine ever used from rockets and jets back through Allison, Packard, and Rolls-Royce to Austro-Daimler, Maybach, Isotta-Fraschini, and an early Curtiss V12. There is an extensive collection of racing photos throughout the museum, and the Trophy Room features a collection of trophies, medals, and personal mementos from around the world.

The museum founder is William R. Tuthill, a noted and versatile pioneer of auto, motorcycle, and stock car racing in the United States, who now preserves the history of speed in his country for the benefit of thousands of enthusiastic visitors.

DATES: Open every day of the year
HOURS: 9 A.M. to 6 P.M.
ADMISSION: Adults $1.25
Ages 8–15 $.75 cents
Under 8 yrs. with adult FREE
Students and servicemen $1.00

CIRCUS HALL OF FAME
Sarasota, Florida

The Circus Hall of Fame was organized in 1954, construction was completed in 1955, and exhibits opened to the public in 1956. This "oldest established circus museum in the Americas" is situated on Highway 41, at Sarasota-Bradenton Airport. There are many special collections, including the largest collection of circus parade Sunburst wagon wheels in the world. Circus trains, models, photographs, posters, and famous wagons are all exhibited. In addition, marionettes perform daily in the puppet theater and professional, live circus acts are featured for visitors from the week before Christmas until the week after Easter, and from the first week in June until Labor Day. Circus greats are nominated annually for enshrinement in the hall of fame by a National Awards Committee. Guided tours are available, and there is a gift shop for souvenirs of your visit. *Holiday, Life, Travel* and *Venture* magazines have praised the Circus Hall of Fame highly, and their recommendation is more than justified.

DATES: Open every day of the year
HOURS: 9 A.M. to 5 P.M. daily

RINGLING MUSEUM OF THE CIRCUS

Sarasota, Florida

John Ringling, youngest of the Ringling Brothers of circus fame, established in Sarasota, Florida, one of the world's most beautiful art museums, filled it with more than 500 great paintings by the old masters of the Baroque era, and then bequeathed this museum, its collection, his fabulous mansion, and his 68-acre landscaped estate to the people of the State of Florida.

Today the Ringling Museums consist of the Ringling Museum of Art, the Asolo Theater, the John Ringling Residence and the Ringling Museum of the Circus. Together they attract more than 500,000 visitors annually, and are an acknowledged cultural center of the Southeast.

John Ringling did not found a circus museum, and it is unlikely that he was aware of the historic importance of circus artifacts. Yet as time went on, it became evident that this should be done, if a significant part of Americana was not to be lost. In 1948, the Ringling Museum of the Circus was established by the State of Florida on the museum grounds, to serve both as a memorial to Ringling and as a treasure house of memorabilia and documents that illustrate the history of the circus "from Rome to Ringling."

Here are displayed the huge bandwagons, wild animal cage wagons, calliopes, and other trappings of the circus in its heyday. A miniature circus parade from the early 1900s is shown around the walls of one room. A scale model diorama of the famous "big top" complete with its three rings and tiny performers is a popular attraction. There is also a recreation of the "backyard" of the circus with blacksmith shop, cookhouse, harness shop, dressing quarters for performers, and a real "clown alley" with props and disguises used by famous clowns over the years.

DATES: Open every day of the year.
HOURS: Monday through Friday 9 A.M. to 10 P.M.
Saturday 9 A.M. to 5 P.M.
Sunday 1 P.M. to 5 P.M.

ADMISSION: Combination ticket for admission to all three museums, $2.50 plus tax
Single admission tickets to:
  Ringling Museum of the Circus, $1.00 plus tax
  Ringling Museum of Art, $1.00 plus tax
  John Ringling Residence, $1.00 plus tax
Children under 12 admitted free at all times

THE INTERNATIONAL SWIMMING HALL OF FAME

Fort Lauderdale, Florida

This magnificent $1.5 million complex was founded in 1965 through a grant of $1 million from the city of Fort Lauderdale, and includes a 4000-seat swimming-diving stadium, a 400-seat auditorium, a unique aquatics library and archives, a museum of aquatic memorabilia, and an area that honors more than 100 swimmers from many countries. The International Swimming Hall of Fame represents swimming, diving, synchronized swimming and aquatic art, water polo, and water safety programs throughout the world. It aims to convert the curiosity of approximately half a million visitors a year into concern for better swimming and water safety.

This nonprofit educational corporation was officially approved by the FINA Congress (97 countries with organized swimming programs) as an International Hall of Fame at the Mexico City Olympic Games in 1968. It exists through private donations and income from admissions, Hall of Fame Library mail order book sales, memberships, souvenir area, national and international swim meets, conventions and programs, and by acting as headquarters for various aquatic groups. The International Swimming Hall of Fame is in use regularly for: the College Swim Coaches Association, the Swim Facility Operators Association, the American Swim Coaches Association, Gold Coast AAU Meetings, the AAU National Men's and Women's Diving Championships, and National Lifeguard Tournaments, among other events. In fact, everyone connected with this first International Hall of Fame has worked to make it one of the most active institutions involved in the heritage of any sport, and one which cannot fail to delight visitors. Its Executive Director, Mr. Buck Dawson, is also the president of the Hall of Fame Directors Association.

HOURS: Olympic Pool and Diving 10 A.M. to 4 P.M. daily

Museum and Library 10 A.M. to 5 P.M. daily
12 noon to 4 P.M. Sunday

ADMISSION: Adults $.80
Students and Children $.40

Adults $1.00
Students and Children $.50
Family Rate $2.50

Lacrosse Hall of Fame (Proposed). (Courtesy Lacrosse Hall of Fame)

The first floor of the National Rifle Association Firearms Museum. (Courtesy NRA Firearms Museum)

The second floor of the National Rifle Association Firearms Museum. (Courtesy NRA Firearms Museum)

Visitors enjoying a performance in the indoor arena. (Courtesy Circus Hall of Fame)

A gift of England's Queen Victoria to Tom Thumb in 1844. This minute coach was pulled by four Shetland ponies. (Courtesy Circus Hall of Fame)

"Two Hemispheres Band Wagon," the largest, most famous band chariot ever built. It required a team of forty horses to lead this wagon. (Courtesy Circus Hall of Fame)

Circus Hall of Fame. (Courtesy Circus Hall of Fame)

Sir Malcolm Cambell's "Bluebird." (Courtesy Museum of Speed, Daytona International Speedway)

The Ringling Museum of the Circus features displays of costumes of famous performers from years past, posters, heralds, and a large collection of memorabilia of the American circus. Ringling Museum grounds, Sarasota, Florida. (Courtesy John and Mable Ringling Museum of the Art)

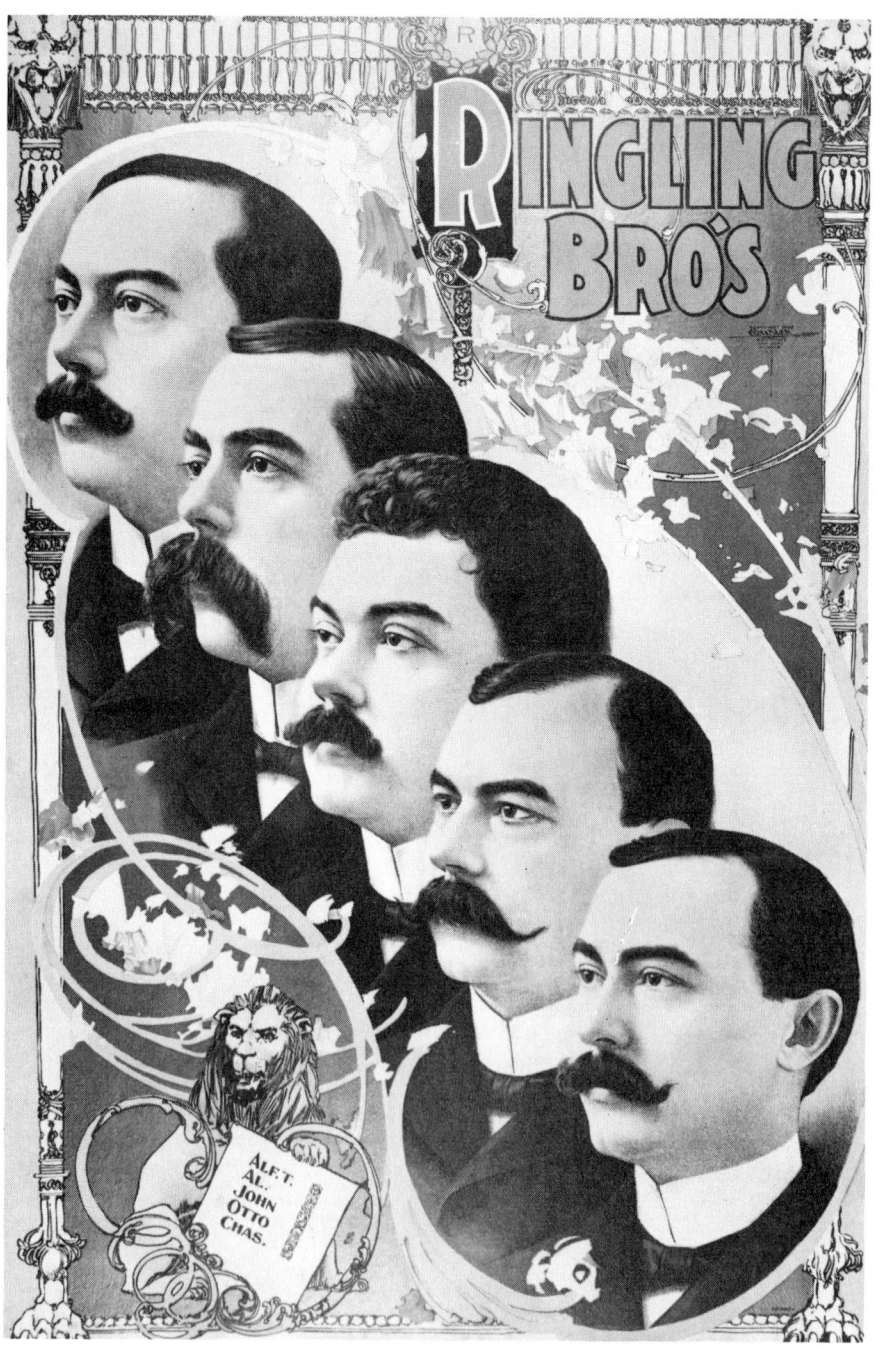

Poster dating back to 1897 shows the five Ringling Brothers who were active in the circus during the years of its founding and expansion. Reading left to right, they are: Alf T., Al, John, Otto and Charles. (Courtesy John and Mable Ringling Museum of the Art)

Southeastern States

"The Five Graces" bandwagon is the oldest circus bandwagon in the United States, having been constructed in 1878 for the Adam Forepaugh Circus. It was later owned by the Barnum & Bailey Circus and toured all of the capitals of Europe, then became the property of Ringling Bros. and Barnum & Bailey. It is one of many magnificent parade wagons in the collection of the Ringling Museum of the Circus, Sarasota, Fla. (Courtesy John and Mable Ringling Museum of the Art)

International Swimming Hall of Fame. (Courtesy International Swimming Hall of Fame)

International Swimming Hall of Fame. (Courtesy International Swimming Hall of Fame)

International Swimming Hall of Fame. (Courtesy International Swimming Hall of Fame)

International Swimming Hall of Fame. (Courtesy International Swimming Hall of Fame)

International Swimming Hall of Fame. (Courtesy International Swimming Hall of Fame)

Johnny Weissmuller, Duke Kahanamoku, and Buster Crabbe were among the first year's honorees. (Courtesy International Swimming Hall of Fame)

Southeastern States

International Swimming Hall of Fame. (Courtesy International Swimming Hall of Fame)

The Joe Weatherly Stock Car Museum. (Courtesy Joe Weatherly Stock Car Museum)

86   SPORTING HERITAGE

The interior of the Joe Weatherly Stock Car Museum. (Courtesy **Joe Weatherly Stock Car Museum**)

Joe Weatherly's 1964 Mercury. (Courtesy Joe Weatherly Stock Car **Museum**)

Southeastern States 87

"Fireball" Roberts' 1963 Ford. (Courtesy Joe Weatherly Stock Car Museum)

"Fireball" Roberts display. (Courtesy Joe Weatherly Stock Car Museum)

Joe Weatherly display. (Courtesy Joe Weatherly Stock Car Museum)

PART IV
Middle Western States

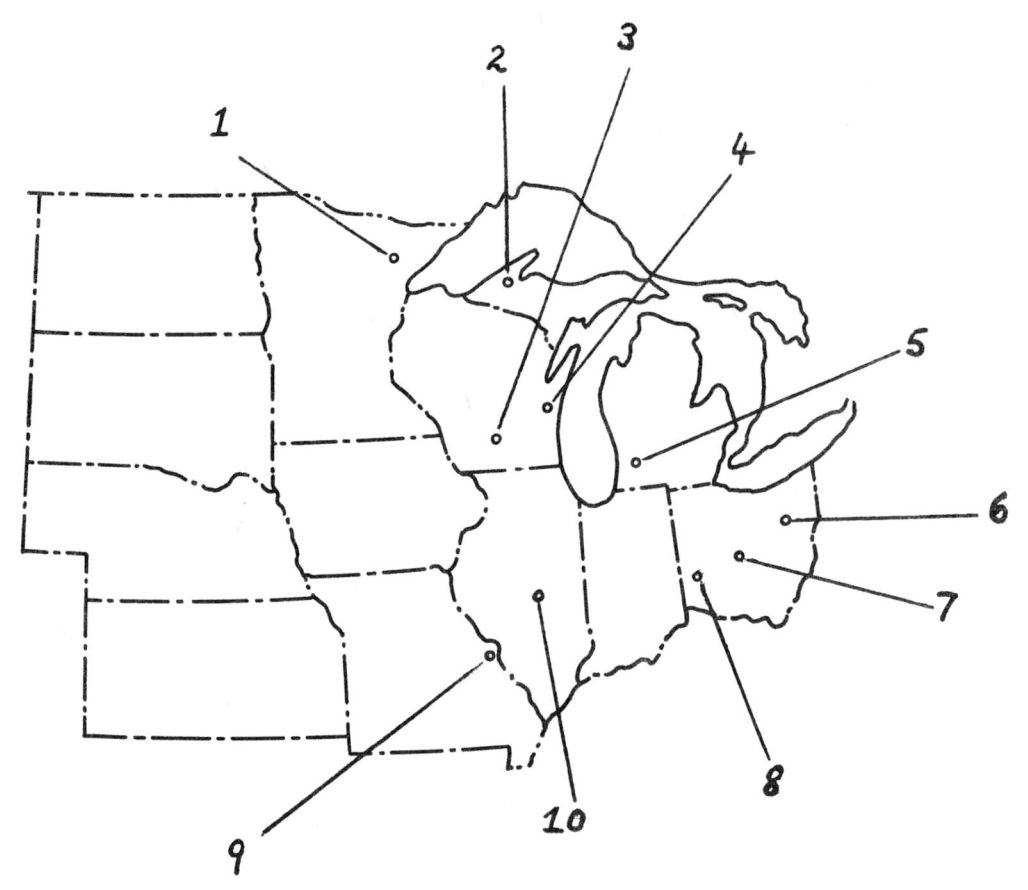

MIDDLE WESTERN STATES

1. United States Hockey Hall of Fame
2. National Ski Hall of Fame
3. Circus World Museum
4. EAA Air Museum
5. AACBC Hall of Fame
6. Pro Football Hall of Fame
7. WIBC Hall of Fame
8. ATA Hall of Fame
9. St. Louis Sports Hall of Fame
10. Indianapolis Motor Speedway Museum

ST. LOUIS SPORTS HALL OF FAME
St. Louis, Missouri 63102

The magnificent Civic Center Busch Memorial Stadium, close to the famous Gateway Arch in downtown St. Louis, provides a wonderful setting for a hall of fame. This is a live-action museum of all St. Louis sports, but with special features on baseball which has a long and outstanding tradition in St. Louis. The opening mural depicts some of this baseball history, such as Von Der Ahe's American Association Browns, pennant winners for four years in a row (1885–1888), and the birth of their descendants, the St. Louis Cardinals, in 1899 when the old team colors were changed from brown to red (the team had moved from the American Association to the National League in 1892). Visitors can also see a scale model of Sportsman's Park as it was for the first Cardinal World Series in 1926, wall drawings of past and present Cardinal and Brown players, and a photographic montage of players and scenes in St. Louis baseball during the twenties and thirties, a color mural of the "Gashouse Gang" showing the Cardinal team of the 1934 World Series, and trophies and mementos of past times. Minitheaters throughout the main room show films of World Series won by the Cardinals from 1926 to 1967. Scenes of St. Louis during the appropriate period are featured outside the theaters.

One of the most impressive displays is the Stan Musial area, a complete collection of his vast number of trophies from his high school playing days, through his great Cardinal career, up until today. The St. Louis Cardinal Roster Room displays the 1967 National League Pennant and World Championship trophy, as well as color transparencies of the players. There is also a picture wall honoring past and present St. Louis sportswriters and announcers.

The All-Sports Room shows the various sports played in St. Louis from earliest times, with displays of basketball, bowling, football, golf, hockey, soccer, and tennis. The AstroTurf Room features a five-minute color movie explaining AstroTurf installation, a cross-section model of the Busch Stadium AstroTurf, and a miniature football field where visitors may walk on the same AstroTurf surface installed on the stadium's playing field. The hall of fame also has a scale model of Civic Center Busch Memorial Stadium, with a color slide presentation showing the stadium in the phases of construction. A bat display surrounds the stadium model.

A tour of the stadium is also available. Apart from a bird's eye view of St. Louis, visitors can take advantage of this 35-minute walking tour during which they view press facilities, the AstroTurf playing field, and learn about the unique features of the stadium: the scoreboard, lighting system, and the movable stands that convert the field for baseball, football, or other events.

CIVIC CENTER BUSCH MEMORIAL STADIUM

Walnut Street side, Between Gates 5 and 6
Open daily from 10 A.M.

HOURS: Stadium Tour (except when day games conflict) 10:00 A.M. to 3:00 P.M.
Hall of Fame (stadium ticket required during games)
Daily, 10:00 A.M. to 5:00 P.M.
Game nights only, 6:00 P.M. to 11:00 P.M.

ADMISSION: Stadium Tour, $1.25 adults, $.60 children
Hall of Fame, $1.25 adults, $.60 children
Combination Tour (when available), $2.00 adults, $1.00 children—children's rates apply under age 16
Special rates for groups by reservation
Telephone: (314) 421-6790

PROFESSIONAL FOOTBALL HALL OF FAME

Canton, Ohio

Slightly more than 10 years ago, the civic campaign was begun in Canton, Ohio, to make that city the home of a Pro Football Hall of Fame. It was in Canton in 1920 that the American Professional Football Association, the forerunner of the National Football League, was organized. The civic drive gained momentum, won approval of the National Football League, staged a fund-raising campaign, obtained donated park land and, by September 7, 1963, pro football had a glistening new hall of fame.

Described as the sport's "historical treasure chest," where most of the events in the long history of pro football are recorded in one form or another, the Pro Football Hall of Fame in 1971 underwent an expansion program that nearly doubled its original size. Now there are three large exhibition areas, two enshrinement areas, a movie theater seating 250 people, an expanded research library, renovated offices, and a new and much larger gift shop. The hall promotes itself as the "on-the-go" spot among American sports shrines and participates as closely as possible in many of the current-day affairs of professional football. The fan making the trip through the hall is encouraged to "take part" in the displays. There are three rear-view movie projectors that can be activated by the push of a button, two selectro-slide machines and several tape recordings of famous voices or events of the past. A different pro football movie in full color is shown every hour. By 1971, 70 members have been enshrined in the Pro Football Hall of Fame, which holds an annual election and then stages an induction ceremony along with a preseason pro game every summer. Attendance has increased rapidly and a record 247,000 fans visited the pro grid shrine in 1972.

DATES:	The hours are the same for weekdays and weekends and the hall is open every day of the year, except Christmas Day.
HOURS:	9 A.M. to 8 P.M. Memorial Day through Labor Day
	9 A.M. to 5 P.M. Labor Day through Memorial Day

WOMAN'S INTERNATIONAL BOWLING CONGRESS HALL OF FAME

Columbus, Ohio

WIBC instituted the Stars of Yesteryear award in 1953. Ten years later the Meritorious Service award was added and the Superior Performance award was initiated in 1964. The three honor groups were officially combined into the WIBC Hall of Fame in 1965.

This is situated in the headquarters of the Congress at 1225 Dublin Road. A large plaque that contains all the names of the women in the WIBC Hall of Fame is in the lobby. A glass display case in the assembly room contains a display of photographs and biographical sketches.

DATES: Monday through Friday
HOURS: 8:30 A.M. to 4:30 P.M.
ADMISSION: FREE

THE A.T.A. HALL OF FAME AND TRAPSHOOTING MUSEUM

The Amateur Trapshooting Association
Permanent Home Grounds,
Vandalia, Ohio

The permanent home grounds of the Amateur Trapshooting Association are maintained for the purpose of holding its annual tournament. This takes place over a period of nine days each August, when more than 4000 trapshooters from the United States and Canada use 53 traps extending for a mile and a quarter on the 97-acre grounds. These contestants are competing in championships for North America, which have been held continuously since 1900.

Before 1924 this series of championships, known as the Grand American Tournament, was held in various places throughout the United States. In that year, however, a clubhouse and trap line were constructed by the association in Vandalia, Ohio, and from then onwards, the Grand American had a permanent home.

As the entries for the tournament increased over the years, the trap line was expanded and other necessary buildings were added. The increase reflected the growing popularity of the sport. In 1968 the association, which governs the largest clay-target sport in the world, improved the clubhouse and added a wing to house the newly-created Hall of Fame and Trapshooting Museum. This was formally opened during the Grand American in August 1969, and celebrates "the history and legend of the great names in trapshooting in North America." Some of these great names include Americans like Captain A. H. ("Adam") Bogardus, W. F. ("Doc") Carver, the famous Annie Oakley, and Sam Vance, "the Father of Trapshooting in Canada." Exhibits depict the historic glass ball era up to the modern trap of today. Various traps and guns are displayed as well as silver trophies dating back to the early years of the sport. A special display features the evolution of the target.

Hall of fame candidates are selected from two groups, contributors and participants. Candidates are eligible for selection after 25 years of participation in the sport.

DATES: Year round
HOURS: 8 A.M. to 4:30 P.M. Monday through Friday

AACBC HALL OF FAME
Kalamazoo, Michigan

Interest in establishing a hall of fame was expressed at the organizational meeting of the American Association of Collegiate Baseball Coaches in 1945, but it was 1965 before a committee was appointed to select a location for the shrine. Installation of the first members of the hall was completed in 1966.

The AACBC Hall of Fame occupies an attractive ground-floor room of the Gary Physical Education Center, Western Michigan University. Fifty-three famous coaches are already honored. Their pictures, and certificates listing their accomplishments, decorate the walls. Minimum requirements for inclusion are that the honoree must have coached college baseball successfully for a minimum of 15 years. Plans are in hand, also, for other exhibits to be included in the future (such as the first baseball ever used in a collegiate game).

DATES: "Visitors are welcome the year round."
ADMISSION: FREE

THE AIR MUSEUM OF THE EXPERIMENTAL AIRCRAFT ASSOCIATION

Franklin, Wisconsin

Officials of the Experimental Aircraft Association began collecting items for the future E.A.A. Air Education Museum in 1955, two years after the founding of the Experimental Aircraft Association. Hundreds of items of importance in illustrating the history of light aircraft were donated by members of the association and others, and in 1964 the Educational Air Museum made the collection available for public viewing.

This $450,000 museum, situated in a fieldstone-fronted rectangular building on a 115-acre tract, is at 11311 West Forest Home Avenue. It exhibits approximately 70 airplanes, depicting the history of flying from the earliest gliders to military jets. One can see, for instance, an 1896 glider, a 1912 Curtiss biplane, a 1917 Newport 14, and an F-86 Sabre jet. Also featured is "the world's smallest aircraft," with a wing span of only 7 feet, 2 inches, and a German Fokker triplane, made famous by the Red Baron (Manfred von Richthofen) himself. Other items on display are: a rare Falker D-9 replica, a world war II Japanese Oscar fighter plane, the Grumman Gulfhawk, one of the first airline aircraft in the country, a Fairchild FC2. Aero engines of all types, "in-line," "opposed," "radial," "rotary," "vee," and jet, are displayed, too. About 100,000 people visited this fascinating air museum last year.

HOURS: 8:30 A.M. to 5 P.M. weekdays
              1 P.M. to 5 P.M. Sundays
ADMISSION: FREE

CIRCUS WORLD MUSEUM

Baraboo, Wisconsin

John M. Kelley began a campaign to interest others in establishing a circus museum in Baraboo, Wisconsin in 1950. Buildings that formerly housed the Ringling Bros. Circus were purchased, and in 1959 the Circus World Museum opened. It is owned by the State Historical Society of Wisconsin. In 1969 the National Park Service of the U.S. Department of the Interior designated the original Ringling Winterquarters buildings as National Historic Landmarks, because of their influential role in American life and culture.

This educational and historic museum is devoted exclusively to the history of circuses of the world. There are 8 huge buildings on 15 acres. In one 400-ft. long building is displayed the world's largest collection of circus parade wagons—over 100 vehicles.

Each July a real circus train packed with the museum's valuable wagons, animals, and wardrobe leaves Baraboo for the sentimental journey through Wisconsin's rolling dairyland to Milwaukee where "The Greatest Circus Parade of All Time" marches through the downtown streets on the Fourth of July to recreate a historic presentation of the old-time circus street parade. Sponsored by the civic-minded Jos. Schlitz Brewing Co., this featured event during "Old Milwaukee Days" annually attracts more than a million people who line the streets as much as eight hours ahead of time to see this refreshing bit of Americana. Millions more watch this colorful and exciting pageant on national television.

The museum's library and archives, with its full-time staff, serves as a clearing house for inquiries on the circus, thus continuing one of the main missions of the museum—the dissemination of circus history. The museum also loans exhibits, lithographs, and other circus artifacts to art centers and similar institutions around the country who are interested in displaying authentic materials on the vanishing outdoor circus.

One can see live, trained animal performances, including elephants, horses, ponies, and dogs, an exciting show of loading and unloading the circus train with draft horses, a daily circus street parade, steam and air calliope, una-fon and band organ concerts, and P. T. Barnum's

Sideshow of the 19th Century. There are also goat cart and pony wagon rides for little tots. Unusual souvenirs can be obtained at the Circus Gift Shop, and refreshments at the Circus Commissary. One admission ticket covers all entertainment and auto parking.

DATES:	Open mid-May to mid-September to the touring public
	Office, library, and workshops are open year-round
HOURS:	9 A.M. to 5:30 P.M. seven days a week
ADMISSION:	Adults $2.25
	Children $.75

NATIONAL SKI HALL OF FAME
Ishpeming, Michigan

The proposal for a hall of fame was first presented by Harold Grinden, President of the National Ski Association, 1928–29, but it was 1944 before the association endorsed the movement. After years of planning the National Convention approved plans for it on May 4, 1950. The building was dedicated in 1954 and the first honorees inducted in 1956.

This $50,000 building measures 34 by 52 feet, and has two floors. All who are interested in this sport will find the National Ski Hall of Fame fascinating and full of items of interest. The different types of skis, so well preserved, are skillfully displayed. So, too, are the trophies.

Featured is an Honor-of-Greatness Display, photo-biographical composites for each of the Ski Hall's Honored 123 Members to date —the display dedicated July 14, 1971. Twelve new members are to be added during the 1971–72 ski season, with photo composites to be framed and hung ahead of the summer tourist season. Despite a budget of less than $8,000 to cover all expenditures within the Ski Hall and Ski Hall Committee work, the National Ski Hall of Fame is kept open the year round thanks to staffing provided through a work aid project grant from Northern Michigan University, Neighborhood Youth Corps assistance in Ishpeming, and the Senior Citizens' Council of Ishpeming—for what may be the most unusual staffing of any sports hall of fame in the nation.

DATES: Open daily mid-June through Labor Day
Wednesday through Sunday weekly the balance of the year
ADMISSION: FREE

UNITED STATES HOCKEY HALL OF FAME

Eveleth, Minnesota

Dedication ceremonies for the recently completed United States Hockey Hall of Fame building are scheduled for June, 1973. Eveleth, a town in which ice hockey is a sport of long-standing tradition, has provided the National Hockey League and other organizations with many players of such calibre as Frank Brimsek, Mike Karakas, Sam Lo Presti, and John Mariucci. Its high school and junior college teams have compiled outstanding records, including five State Championships for the high school, and four of its sons were members of the 1956 Olympic team.

The proposal that Eveleth should sponsor the construction of a hockey hall of fame facility originated with the Project H Committee of the Eveleth Civic Association. In 1968, the Amateur Hockey Association of the United States officially endorsed Eveleth as the hall of fame site. Funding of the project was greatly aided by a grant from the Federal Economic Development Administration and a $100,000 gift from the National Hockey League.

In this magnificent building there will be an area to honor those Americans who have made important contributions to the sport as players, coaches, referees, and administrators. In addition, there will be display areas for the various categories of hockey as played in the United States, high school, amateur, college, professional and international. Also included in the plans are provisions for a library, theater, and souvenir shop.

THE INDIANAPOLIS MOTOR SPEEDWAY MUSEUM

Indianapolis, Indiana

The Indianapolis Motor Speedway Museum is located in the east wing of the office building at the main entrance to the grounds of the speedway, which incorporates a 2.5-mile race course inside a 539-acre site, and is the home of the world-famous Indianapolis 500-mile race. The track was opened for racing in 1909, and the first 500-mile Classic was held in 1911. Since then the story has been one of continuous expansion and improvement to the status that the "Indy 500" enjoys today as one of the world's greatest sports events.

The museum was opened in 1956, just prior to the great race, and contains an interesting display of exhibits that have contributed to the history of this renowned event for the past 62 years. In addition to many photos and trophies, eighteen famous cars are on display including eleven "500" winners. Visitors can see the Marmon Wasp in which Ray Harroun won the first 500 in 1911, the Duesenberg that Jimmy Murphy drove to Victory Lane in 1922 and with which he won the French Grand Prix at Le Mans, and the Sheraton-Thompson Special in which A. J. Foyt, Jr. scored his 1964 triumph. Other famous cars from England, France, Germany, and Italy are also featured in the speedway display. Etchings of each 500-mile race winner form an impressive display in the center of the museum, accompanied by a huge plaque honoring all members of Auto Racing's Hall of Fame, and many other mementos.

The museum has been improved continuously since it was first opened to the public, and conscientious research and development have provided new items for display, including many other cars. There is no doubt that it is already one of the most unique and complete institutions of its kind and a national showplace for thousands of delighted visitors.

DATES: Daily
HOURS: 9 A.M. to 5 P.M.
ADMISSION: FREE

The main room of the Hall of Fame features wall drawings of famous Cardinal and Brown players, photographic montages of baseball in the '20s and '30s, and a color mural of the 1934 Gashouse Gang. Round cylinders spaced throughout the room are minitheaters which show films of World Series won by the Cardinals from 1926-1967. (Courtesy Robert Artega, Artega Photos, St. Louis)

Aerial view of Civic Center Busch Memorial Stadium, home of the St. Louis Sports Hall of Fame.

Aerial photograph of the downtown St. Louis area showing Civic Center Busch Memorial Stadium and the Gateway Arch.

A section of the St. Louis Sports Hall of Fame is devoted to Stan Musial and his many awards. (Courtesy Robert Artega, Artega Photos, St. Louis)

Middle Western States

Hall of Fame guide, Dotty Williams, looking at part of the extensive collection of Stan Musial's trophies and mementos. (Courtesy Mack Giblin Photography)

A very impressive and complete collection of Stan Musial's trophies and mementos, showing guide Dotty Williams looking at Stan's famous No.6 uniform.

Middle Western States 107

Stan Musial addressed crowd during the third anniversary party held at the Hall of Fame in June, 1971. Shown in photograph, left to right, are Bing Devine, general manager of the St. Louis Cardinals; Jackie Jordan, director of the Sports Hall of Fame; C. C. Johnson Spink, editor and publisher of the Sporting News; and Stan Musial.

Professional Football Hall of Fame. (Courtesy Professional Football Hall of Fame)

Ramp leading to exhibition rotunda. (Courtesy Professional Football Hall of Fame)

Actual Hall of Fame area. (Courtesy Professional Football Hall of Fame)

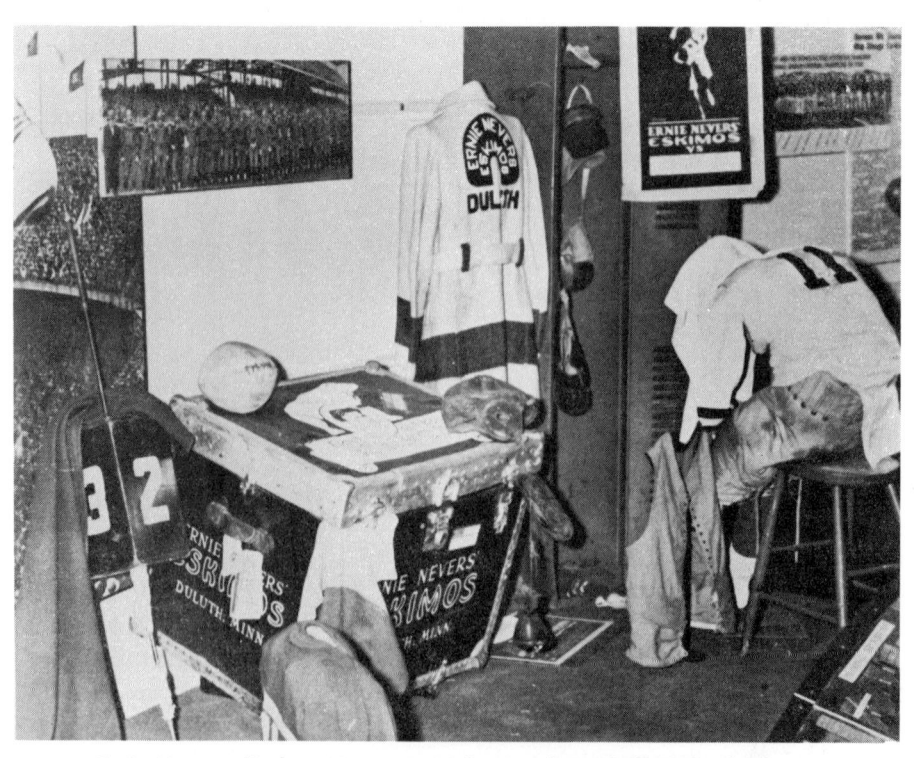

Ernie Nevers display. (Courtesy Professional Football Hall of Fame)

Jim Thorpe display. (Courtesy Professional Football Hall of Fame)

Temporary enshrinement area—1968 class. (Courtesy Professional Football Hall of Fame)

Display of team helmets. (Courtesy Professional Football Hall of Fame)

The Air Museum of the Experimental Aircraft Association. (Courtesy Experimental Aircraft Assoc.)

Middle Western States

Air Museum of the Experimental Aircraft Association. (Courtesy A. L. Schmidt)

Circus World Museum. (Courtesy Circus World Museum)

A view of a small portion of the 15-acre lot covered by the Circus World Museum in Baraboo, Wisconsin. The domed building on the right is the Hippodrome, in which the circus performances are presented twice each day. (Courtesy Circus World Museum)

Middle Western States 115

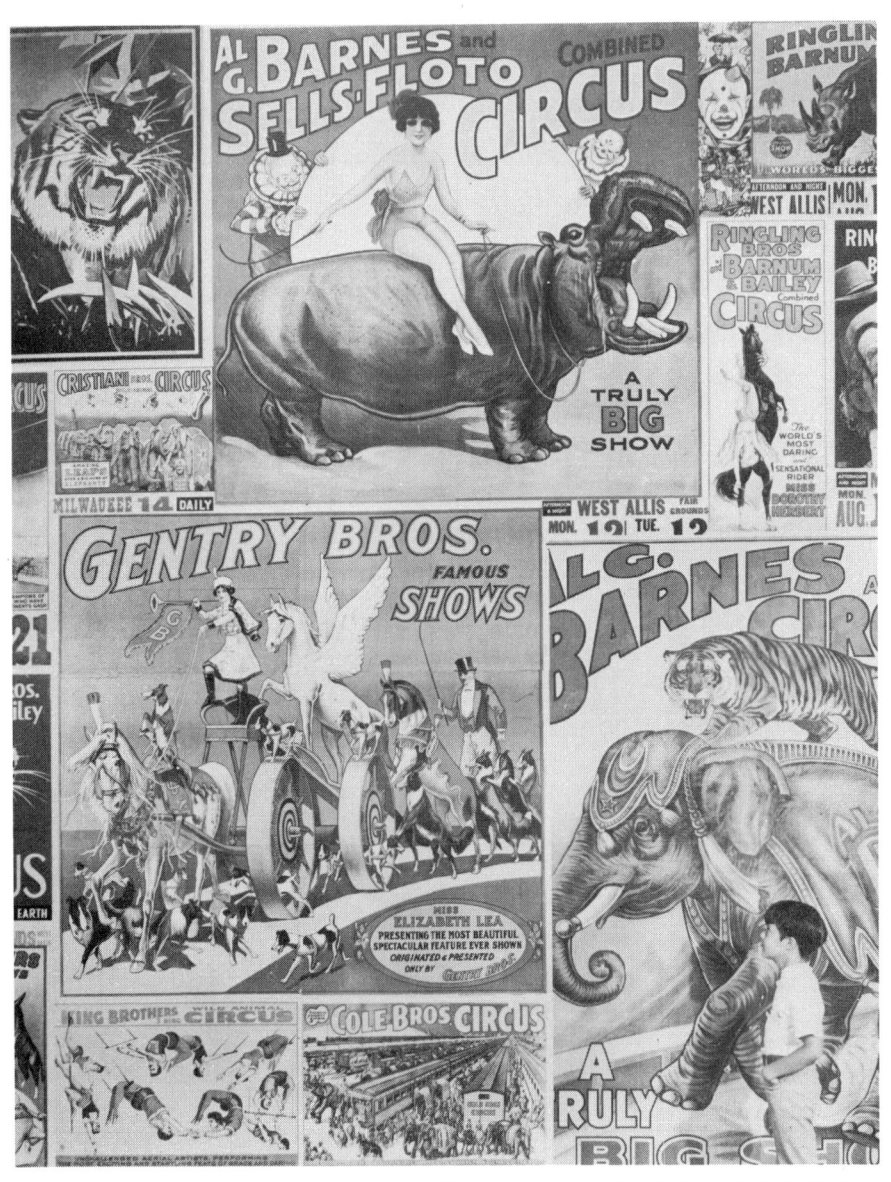

All the famous circuses of years gone by are memorialized in colorful displays at the museum. This beautiful splash of color is being admired by Joel Parkinson who has his eye on the dogs and ponies. (Courtesy Circus World Museum)

A six-horse team of dapple grey Percherons pull wagon 55 at the museum. The wagon contains a lusty sounding Wurlitzer military band-organ. (Courtesy Circus World Museum)

Eight beautiful Percherons—eight tons of powerful horses perform daily. They work loading a circus train, pulling water wagons, and as a grand 8-horse team pulling a huge circus parade wagon. Pictured here they are taking a short rest in the circus tent stable—shades of 50 years ago when the big circuses carried 200 to 300 of these magnificent horses to do all the work. (Courtesy Circus World Museum)

Middle Western States

The sound of the circus—the steam calliope—can be heard for a distance of five miles. It is played daily in concerts. (Courtesy Circus World Museum)

And, of course, the elephants do their thing. (Courtesy Circus World Museum)

Library and Research Center, Circus World Museum, Baraboo, Wisconsin. (Courtesy Circus World Museum)

National Ski Hall of Fame.

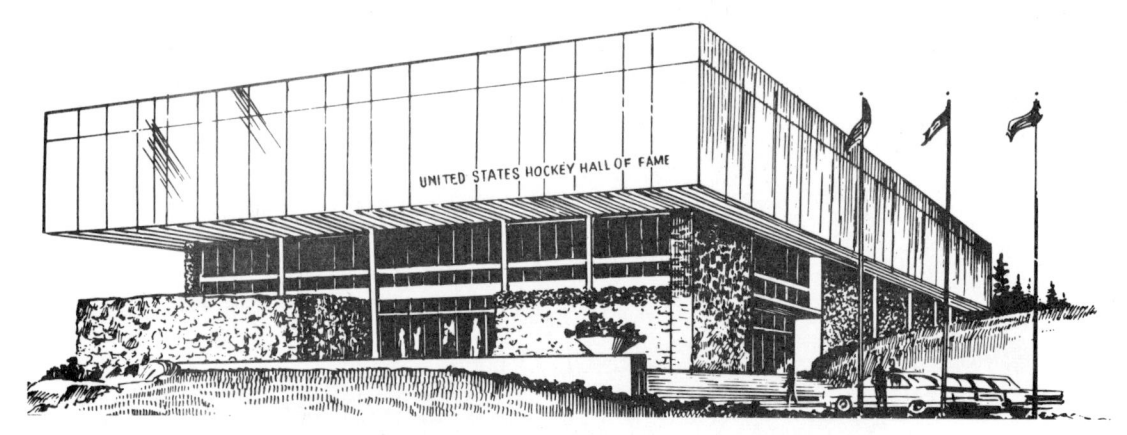

United States Hockey Hall of Fame. (Courtesy U.S. Hockey Hall of Fame)

The Indianapolis Motor Speedway Museum. (Courtesy Indianapolis Motor Speedway)

Interior of the Indianapolis Motor Speedway. (Courtesy Indianapolis Motor Speedway)

PART V
Southwestern States

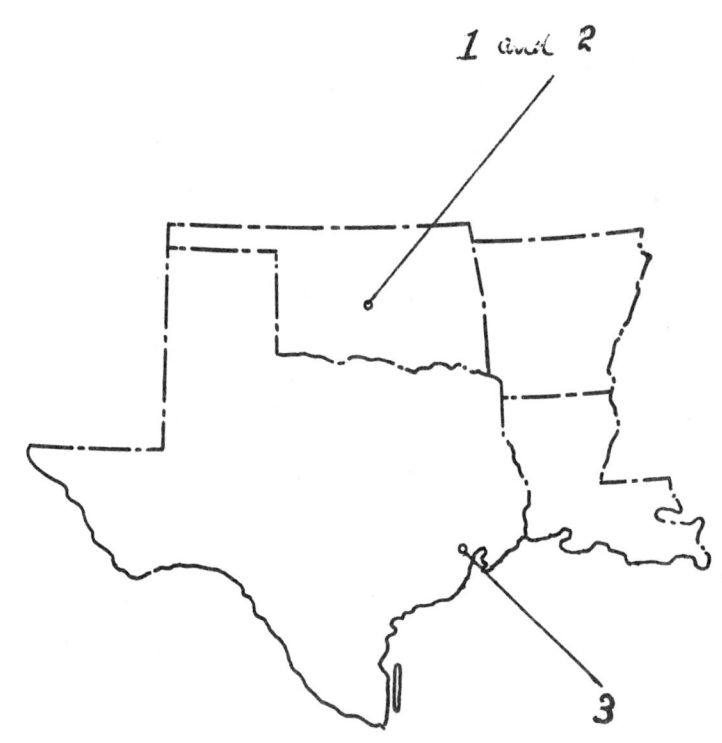

SOUTHWESTERN STATES

1. National Cowboy Hall of Fame and Western Heritage Center
2. Amateur Softball Association Hall of Fame
3. Houston Baseball Museum

NATIONAL COWBOY HALL OF FAME AND WESTERN HERITAGE CENTER

Oklahoma City, Oklahoma

Chester A. Reynolds, a Kansas City garment manufacturer, conceived the idea for the cowboy museum after visiting the Will Rogers memorial in Claremore, Oklahoma, in 1952. He personally arranged for the creation of an interstate commission, with representatives from seventeen states. The commission drafted plans for the shrine and raised the funds necessary to construct, equip, and maintain the museum. It opened on June 26, 1965.

This magnificent museum, housing a western art and history collection valued at five million dollars, is situated on 37-acre Persimmon Hill. The flags of 17 western states, plus the Stars and Stripes, fly at the entrance. There are famous guns, saddles, and all types of western memorabilia. Life-sized dioramas illuminate the past—the cowboys and Indians, trappers and traders, and cavalrymen. Visitors can admire the famous Matador Ranch Chuckwagon and an exact copy of the Butterfield Overland Mail Stage, as well as the Great Map, a 32-by-48-foot relief map enclosed in a small auditorium, illustrating all the trails west. A large collection of western art by Charles Russell, Frederic Remington, Thomas Moran, W. R. Leigh, Charles Schreyvogel, and many others, is featured. The Fraser Studio Collection of great American sculpture is an important addition, and includes the West's most famous statue, by James Fraser, named *The End of the Trail*. Rodeo cowboys are honored in the National Rodeo Hall of Fame. Many others, such as Will Rogers, "Buffalo Bill," "Kit" Carson, and Gary Cooper, are honored in the Hall of Fame of Great Westerners. Nearly two million visitors have already appreciated this supreme example of the preservation of a heritage. It is situated at 1700 Northeast 63rd Street, overlooking U.S. Highway 66.

DATES: Open daily
HOURS: 9:30 A.M. to 5:30 P.M.
Memorial Day to Labor Day, 8:30 A.M. to 6 P.M.
ADMISSION: Christmas Day and Thanksgiving, 1 P.M. to 5:30 P.M.
Adults $1.00   Children (under 13) $.50
"Pre-schoolers" are FREE. Special rates for groups.

NATIONAL SOFTBALL HALL OF FAME

Oklahoma City, Oklahoma, Off Route I-35

Construction on a $300,000 building that will house the National Softball Hall of Fame, national headquarters for the Amateur Softball Association of America, and offices of the International Softball Federation began early in May, 1971. Presently 39 former players have been elected to the shrine. In addition to detailing their accomplishments and contributions, the hall will serve to focus attention on all important developments that have taken place in the history of softball. The building is located less than one mile from the Cowboy Hall of Fame.

THE HOUSTON BASEBALL MUSEUM

Houston, Texas

Arthur M. Meyer, Sr., of Houston, a department store executive, began his collection of autographed baseballs and other memorabilia in 1940. In 1968, the artifacts of other items of historic interest were made available for public viewing in the Houston Baseball Museum.

This is located on the site of the home plate of historic Buffalo Stadium in the Finger Furniture Center, 4001 Gulf Freeway, at Cullen Boulevard. The museum features in the collection souvenirs from Babe Ruth, Stan Musial, the Walker Brothers and others, an original sheet music copy of "Take Me Out To The Ball Game," autographed by the composer, Jack Northworth, and baseballs with the autographs of three United States presidents: Herbert Hoover, Harry S. Truman, and Dwight D. Eisenhower. The physical structure of the museum is a replica of the famous Houston Astrodome, and the interior features a panoramic view "of old Buff Stadium, a symbol of baseball to three generations of Houstonians."

DATES: Open daily, except Sundays
HOURS: 10 A.M. to 9 P.M. Mondays to Fridays
10 A.M. to 6 P.M. Saturdays
ADMISSION: FREE

Southwestern States

The End of the Trail by James Earle Fraser. The original 1915 plaster statue was made for the Panama-Pacific International Exposition held in San Francisco in that year. It is now located in the Fraser collection here. (Courtesy National Cowboy Hall of Fame and Western Heritage Center)

National Cowboy Hall of Fame and Western Heritage Center. (Courtesy National Cowboy Hall of Fame and Western Heritage Center)

National Cowboy Hall of Fame and Western Heritage Center. (Courtesy National Cowboy Hall of Fame and Western Heritage Center)

Southwestern States 131

National Cowboy Hall of Fame and Western Heritage Center. (Courtesy National Cowboy Hall of Fame and Western Heritage Center)

View of the National Rodeo Hall of Fame in this complex. A bronze statue of Bill Linderman, by Bob Scriver, is in the foreground. (Courtesy National Cowboy Hall of Fame and Western Heritage Center)

(Courtesy Amateur Softball Association)

PART VI

Rocky Mountain and West Coast States

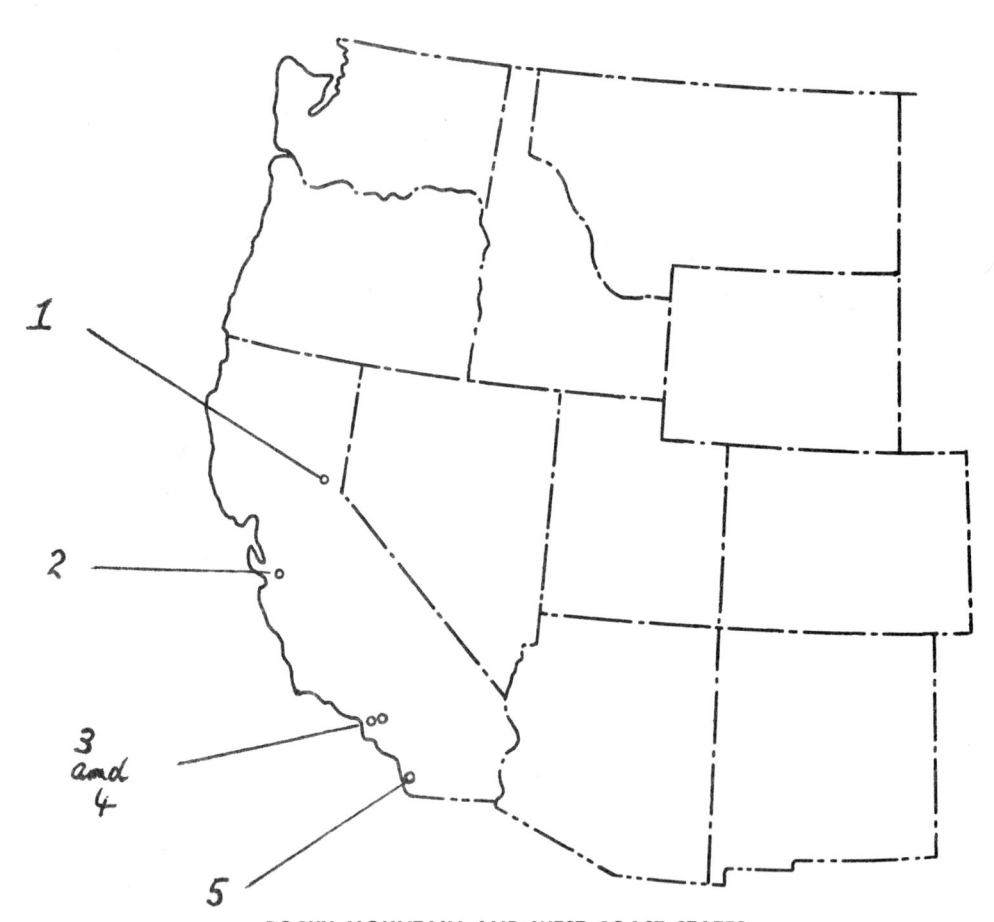

ROCKY MOUNTAIN AND WEST COAST STATES

1. Western America Skisport Museum
2. San Jose State College Sports Library
3. Helms Hall
4. Rose Bowl Hall of Fame
5. San Diego Hall of Champions

WESTERN AMERICA SKISPORT MUSEUM

Boreal Ridge Ski Area
Donner Summit—Highway I-80, California

The Western America Skisport Museum opened its doors to the public following dedication ceremonies held on December 7, 1969. Its existence is due mainly to the efforts of the membership and leadership of the Auburn (California) Ski Club, President Wendell T. Robie designer of the building, and the contributions of William B. Berry, museum historian. The ski area is visited by more than 100,000 persons annually, many of whom also tour the Skisport Museum.

Largest of the displays is that of the Alturas Snowshoe Club. Founded in 1867, the Alturas Club was the first organization formed for the purpose of staging championship ski racing. Also, there are displays of activities, both past and present, of the Auburn Ski Club, the United States Forest Service, the National Ski Patrol System, the 10th Mountain Division of World War II, the Reno Ski Club, the Lake Tahoe Ski Club, the United States Ski Association, and the United States Olympic Association. One may also see a pair of antique "snow skates," attributed to John A. ("Snow-Shoe") Thompson, and a leather mailbag actually used by the pioneering skiing expressman on his trans-Sierra routes over 100 years ago.

The Skisport Museum also houses a nondenominational chapel on its second floor. Here Catholic Mass is held each Sunday during the ski season, Protestant Sunday School groups use it on other occasions, and it is also a meeting place for ski instructors, ski patrolmen, ski club members, and intercollegiate and interscholastic ski team groups and coaches.

DATES: Open Wednesday through Sunday
ADMISSION: FREE

SAN JOSE STATE COLLEGE SPORTS LIBRARY

San Jose, California

This library houses the collection of Fred Imhof of San Jose, California, which was the result of many years' work. It is described in the *Guinness Book of World Records* as the world's largest privately-owned collection of its type. Illness compelled Imhof to sell the collection to a California corporation, Sports Expert, Inc., headed by San Jose *Mercury* sportswriter, Wes Mathis. The collection is housed at San Jose State College under a special contract between the college and corporation, which allows access to the collection by authorized scholars. (Arrangements for access can be made by writing to W. F. Gustafson at San Jose State College.)

Only a brief, and therefore inadequate, description of this unique collection can be given here. There are books, journals and periodicals, almanacs and guides, game programs, and magazine and newspaper clippings. All references to a particular sport are shelved together, and every sport imaginable is included, from the well known to the unusual.

UNITED SAVINGS–HELMS ATHLETIC FOUNDATION
AND
UNITED SAVINGS–HELMS HALL

9800 South Sepulveda Boulevard
Los Angeles, California

In 1936 Paul H. Helms established the Helms Athletic Foundation, a philanthropic institution, serving in the interest of sports. The concept for the athletic foundation was that of W. R. Bill Schroeder, who became the managing director, and has been since 1936.

Original offices were in the William May Garland Building, Los Angeles, and remained until 1948.

Paul H. Helms, prominent Los Angeles business man and civic leader, and his family, provided the funds that were necessary for the operation of the athletic foundation and its extensive awards program. Helms passed away in 1957, but his family continued to support the foundation.

The Helms family erected Helms Hall, international sports shrine, in 1948, dedicated on October 17. It then housed the headquarters of Helms Athletic Foundation and its massive sports library, considered to be the largest in existence. It was designed specifically as a sports museum.

Lodged in Helms Hall were the awards won and entrusted by famed athletes, photographs of champions and championship teams, and a countless number of sports artifacts. Visitation, without admission charge, exceeds 50,000 annually.

Adjoining the hall was a spacious outdoor, but covered, patio, with a huge fireplace. It was here, in charming but informal setting, that hundreds of awards programs, luncheons, and dinners, as well as delightful parties, were held with noted athletes, coaches, and sports dignitaries (many from foreign lands) attending, frequently being honored guests.

Helms awards included those for athletes of the year, and month, all-America and championship teams in major categories, and those who excelled in high school and junior ranks.

In 1948, upon completion of Helms Hall, a hall of fame program was developed for many sports, citing athletes, coaches and noteworthy contributors.

The internationally known World Trophy awards were instituted in 1949, which served to recognize the foremost amateur athletes of Africa, Asia, Australasia, Europe, and North and South America each year, as selections were dated back to the year 1896, when the first of the modern Olympic games were held at Athens, Greece.

Although the sparkling trophy and medal cases, and pictorial panels captured the eyes of visitors, the two focal points in Helms Hall were the huge World Trophy of gold and silver, set upon a green marble base, bearing the names of all of those who had been honored since 1896, and the glittering Olympic Room, in which were placed the awards won and entrusted by Olympic Games medalists.

The athletic foundation's Olympic Games collection is believed to be the most complete extant.

On July 1, 1970, the Helms family found it impossible to continue as the benefactor of the athletic foundation and sports shrine, which was located on Venice Boulevard in West Los Angeles.

For a few months in 1970, the athletic foundation and sports shrine were in a semirest period, although the managing director carried on his activities, as a new benefactor was sought. There were a number of impressive offers, nationwide, although the managing director preferred to remain in Southern California.

Finally, in September of 1970, United Savings and Loan Association of California offered to serve as the continuing and permanent benefactor of the athletic foundation and sports shrine. This offer was looked upon favorably by the managing director, for he had worked closely with United Savings and Loan Association in connection with a U.S. Olympic Fund program in 1968, and successfully so. Through this association, the managing director had created warm friendships with executives of United Savings and Loan Association, particularly with Elwood A. Teague, chairman of the Board.

Subsequently, Elwood A. Teague, on behalf of his Board of Directors, and W. R. Bill Schroeder agreed that United Savings and Loan Association would become the continuing and permanent benefactor of the athletic foundation and sports shrine, as they would be known as United Savings Helms Athletic Foundation, and United Savings Helms Hall. This became a reality on October 6, 1970, as the Helms family gave its blessings.

For eight months, there was a redevelopment program, as the

countless number of trophies, awards, artifacts, plaques, photographs, and the sports library were moved from the old location on Venice Boulevard, to the new one, 9800 South Sepulveda Boulevard, Los Angeles.

The grand opening of United Savings Helms Hall, and United Savings Helms Athletic Foundation, in their charming new quarters, was held on July 26, 1971, as more than 1200 noted athletes, coaches, sportsmen, and civic leaders were in attendance.

As has been the situation for years, the athletic foundation and sports shrine enjoy the cooperation of two boards to act upon awards selections: The United Savings Helms Hall Awards Board, of which Elwood A. Teague is the chairman (World Trophy, Halls of Fame, Athlete of the Year, Athlete of the Month, and special awards), and the All Southern California Board of Athletics (high school awards).

HOURS: 9 A.M. to 5 P.M. Monday through Friday
9 A.M. to 3 P.M. Saturdays, excepting holidays
ADMISSION: FREE

THE ROSE BOWL HALL OF FAME

Tournament House, 391 South Orange Grove Boulevard, Pasadena, California 91105

Tournament House is a mansion that formerly belonged to the Wrigley Chewing Gum Company. The exhibit of photographs and other material was moved there from the Rose Bowl when construction alterations made the previous location unavailable. Tournament House and the Rose Bowl Room are open every Wednesday afternoon to the public. There is no admission charge.

SAN DIEGO HALL OF CHAMPIONS
Balboa Park, San Diego, California 92101

The San Diego Hall of Champions is a nonprofit corporation involved in the promotion of educational work with particular reference to athletics and physical education. It has attracted more than a million-and-a-half visitors since it opened in January, 1961. It operates a public exhibition hall (museum) at 1439 El Prado in Balboa Park, in which are displayed many of the trophies won and sports equipment used by San Diego area athletes who earned national fame and recognition. Some 1400 pictures of these athletes are on view. At the rear center of the museum is a beautifully appointed room that houses the San Diego Hall of Fame, and displays the mounted portraits of 34 famous local athletes.

A film library is also in operation that has over 350 films on various sports. These are available for showing at no charge to groups such as athletic teams, recreation centers, church groups, school classes, and other sports groups. During the past eight years more than 625,000 viewers have used this service. A conference room on the second floor of the museum is also maintained for free use by any cultural or sports group. This conference room was used more than a hundred times in 1972, during which year alone a total of 166,895 persons visited the San Diego Hall of Champions from every state and nineteen foreign countries.

The museum is supported by grants and contributions from the City of San Diego, San Diego County, and public subscriptions. Members of the public can also "sponsor" individuals elected to the Hall of Fame. Contributions also support all capital improvements, such as new displays, which are made in the Hall. No visit to Balboa Park would be complete without enjoying the facilities offered in this worthwhile project.

DATES: Daily. Closed only on Thanksgiving Day, Christmas Day, and New Year's Day.
HOURS: 10 A.M. to 5 P.M. Monday through Saturday.
12 noon to 5 P.M. Sunday
ADMISSION: FREE

Western America Skisport Museum. (Courtesy Skisport Museum)

TV covered the grand opening of United Savings Helms Hall, international sports shrine, on July 26, 1971, as hundreds of invited guests attended. This is a part of the football section of the sports shrine. (Courtesy Helms Hall)

United Savings Helms Hall officials welcome guests at grand opening of the sports shrine, July 26, 1971. Left to right: Elwood A. Teague, Chairman; Bill Schroeder, Managing Director; Jan Iverson, Executive Secretary. (Courtesy Helms Hall)

Mrs. Ralph De Palma, widow of the famed automobile racing driver, points to the trophies which were won by her late husband, lodged in United Savings Helms Hall, international sports shrine. Managing Director Bill Schroeder, looks on. (Courtesy Helms Hall)

The Rose Bowl Football Game, Pasadena, California. (Courtesy Rose Bowl Hall of Fame)

The Tournament of Roses, Pasadena. (Courtesy Rose Bowl Hall of Fame)

The Rose Bowl Football Game, Pasadena. (Courtesy Rose Bowl Hall of Fame)

The San Diego Hall of Champions, California. (Courtesy San Diego Hall of Champions)

The swimming exhibit at the San Diego Hall of Champions. (Courtesy San Diego Hall of Champions)

A football exhibit at the San Diego Hall of Champions. (Courtesy San Diego Hall of Champions)

The basketball, boxing, and wrestling exhibit at the San Diego Hall of Champions. (Courtesy San Diego Hall of Champions)

The Hall of Fame at the San Diego Hall of Champions. (Courtesy San Diego Hall of Champions)

PART VII
Canada

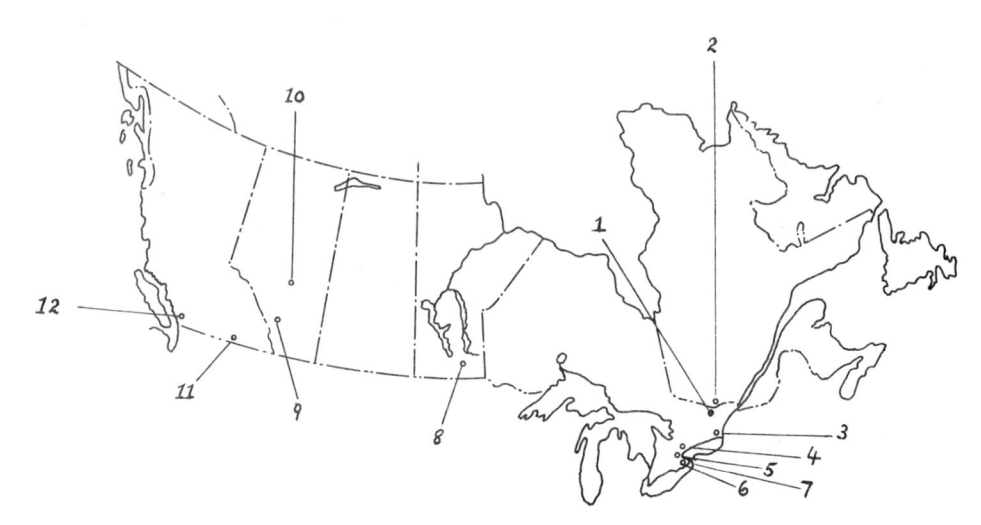

CANADA

1. National Ski Museum
2. Canadian Golf Museum
3. International Hockey Hall of Fame
4. Canada Sports and Hockey Hall of Fame
5. Canadian Football Hall of Fame
6. K. A. Auty Memorial Library
7. Daredevil Hall of Fame
8. Aquatic Hall of Fame
9. Horseman's Hall of Fame
10. Edmonton Hall of Fame
11. British Columbia Ski Hall of Fame
12. British Columbia Sports Hall of Fame

THE CANADIAN GOLF MUSEUM, KINGSWAY PARK, MOUNTAIN ROAD, AYLMER EAST

Quebec

The Canadian Golf Museum and Historical Institute is situated in the stone Clubhouse (circa 1812) of the Kingsway Golf and Country Club at Lucerne, Quebec, and adjacent to the Mackenzie King Estate in Gatineau Park. It contains the private collection of William Lyn Stewart, president of Glenlea Enterprises Limited, which owns and operates this club and also the Glenlea Golf Club. The collection contains items from North America and the United Kingdom, and may be classified into three categories: equipment, books, and prints.

Many excellent examples of nineteenth-century clubs are displayed in cases, including a leather-faced spoon by Willie Park, winner of the first British Open in 1860. Improved irons and hickory-shafted clubs of the early 20th century are also featured, including an iron club by J. H. Oke, winner of the first Canadian Open in 1904. Another case shows various examples of golf club development up to the present-day matched sets of 14 clubs. The evolution of the golf ball is well depicted, from the "feathery" (1830), the "gutty" (1848), the rubber core ball (1898), to the high compression ball of today. A novel item here is a wooden ball improvised in North Africa during the First World War.

Old golf prints adorn the walls of the museum, and the Golf Gallery contains several autographed pictures of champions such as Francis Ouimet, Bobby Jones, Gene Sarazen, Margaret Masters, and Gary Cowan, Canadian Holder of the United States Amateur Championship. Numerous volumes on golf are found in the library, including a rare set of three by the "Triumvirate" of Braid, Taylor, and Vardon.

The Canadian Golf Museum is a registered member of the Canadian Museums Association, and has been approved as a centennial project by the Centennial Commission. It is open daily and there is no admission charge.

THE INTERNATIONAL HOCKEY HALL OF FAME and MUSEUM

Alfred and York Street (Next to Kingston Memorial Centre), Kingston, Ontario

Hockey fans or historians of the game will find something of interest at The International Hockey Hall of Fame and Museum in Kingston, midway between the two sporting centers of Toronto and Montreal.

The shrine, opened in 1965 after a 20-year campaign by local hockey officials, mixes Gordie Howe's gloves, sweater, and stick with relics and pictures of Stanley Cup and amateur champions dating back to the 1890s.

The "International" in the official name of the hall, is authentic. On display is a unique bronze urn, presented to Battleford (Saskatchewan) Millers, the first team to tour Japan (in 1934), Dit Clapper's No. 5 sweater, retired by the Boston Bruins in 1947, a hockey stick from Russia, a pennant from Norway, and pictures of the first professional hockey team in the world from Houghton, Michigan.

Bobby Orr is not eligible for the hall of fame as yet, but his electrifying goal that gave Boston the Stanley Cup in 1970 against St. Louis Blues is recorded in a huge wall poster. Color shots of today's greats, including Phil Esposito and Frank Mahovlich, plus caricatures of the current all-stars and trophy winners are also featured.

One display that attracts hockey fans of all ages, is the collection of cards from the teams of the National Hockey League expansion era to the first cards ever issued when Lester Patrick, Art Ross, and Cyclone Taylor played in the fledgling four-team National Hockey Association. These 60-year-old cards, issued by a tobacco company, are valued today at $5 each.

An outstanding collection of skates tells an early story of Canada's recreation and the progress of the game and its equipment. They range from the crude wooden and iron implements of a century ago to the battered blades of Hall of Fame referee Mike Rodden, and the first hockey "tube" introduced into eastern Canada by Jack Marshall of Montreal's "Little Men of Iron" 70 years ago.

A special corner is reserved for the "hockeyana" of the Kingston man who conceived the idea of a hall of fame for the great winter sport, Capt. James T. Sutherland. A player, manager, referee, and president of the Ontario Hockey Association and Canadian Amateur Hockey Association, he promoted Kingston as the place where shinny grew into hockey and helped convince the CAHA and NHL that this city was the central site for a hockey memorial, in 1943. He died before the Kingston shrine or the NHL sponsored Toronto Hall was opened.

Near the Sutherland showcase are pictures of the annual Kingston Winter Carnival historic hockey game, the recreation of the Royal Military College-Queen's College game played on harbor ice in 1886. Replicas of the field hockey type of stick used in that game are among the souvenirs at the Kingston hall.

The Tommy Gorman collection of pictures of great Ottawa teams graphically illustrate the uniforms and light protective equipment of the days of seven-man hockey.

The main feature of the Kingston hall is the gallery of enshrined members, pictures, and accounts of the top amateur and professional stars of Canada and the United States, plus builders of the game and referees.

HOURS:	July and August, 2 P.M. to 5 P.M. & 7 P.M. to 9 P.M. daily and weekends, Sept. to June, weekends, 2 P.M. to 5 P.M. & 7 P.M. to 9 P.M.
	Special tours on request
ADMISSION:	Adults $.50, students $.25
	Children under 12 free, family rate $1.00
CURATOR:	J. W. Fitsell, 91 Toronto Street, Apt. 5, Kingston, Ont.

CANADA'S SPORTS HALL OF FAME AND HOCKEY HALL OF FAME

Exhibition Park, Toronto 2B

Canada's Sports Hall of Fame was founded on June 10, 1955, largely through the efforts of Mr. Harry Price, then vice-president, and chairman of the Canadian National Exhibition Sports Committee. It was felt that such an institution was needed to fully honor Canada's great athletes. Each province was represented on the Selection Committee in order that the hall should be representative of the whole Dominion.

Historical pictures and records were first accommodated in the Stanley Barracks building until a more suitable location could be obtained, and showings took place at the exhibition's annual fair. In 1957, the Sports Hall of Fame was moved to the Administration Building and occupied half the lower floor. Public patronage of the project led to the usage of the entire ground floor sharing it with the newly-founded Hockey Hall of Fame. The National Hockey League had invited the CNE to a joint investigation of the possibility of combining a Hockey Hall of Fame and Sports Hall of Fame in the same building. Through the cooperation of Mr. Price and his colleagues, a large room in the Sports Hall of Fame was made available for hockey displays. The new building for the Hockey Hall of Fame was completed on May 1, 1961, after an agreement between the NHL, the CNE, and the City of Toronto, and the Canada Sports Hall of Fame is now located in this also.

To date, there are 161 honored members of Canada's Sports Hall of Fame, qualified in many different categories of sports under five main headings: (a) General (basketball, baseball, golf, soccer, tennis, etc.), (b) Track and Field (hurdles, marathon, sprints, etc.), (c) Water Sports (rowing, sailing, swimming, etc.), (d) Winter Sports (bobsled, curling, hockey, skating, skiing, etc.), and (e) All-Round athletes. Five are included in the latter section: Lionel Conacher, F. (Bobbie) Rosenfeld, Walter Knox, R. A. (Bobby) Porter, and Donald H. (Dan) Bain. Any Canadian who wins an Olympic Gold Medal is automatically admitted to the hall. Others who "bring fame to Canada, either as a participant or official" can be elected by the Selection Committee. "Veterans" who have been inactive for at least 20 years, and "builders" who are not competitors or officials, can be honored by the same stipulation. Canada's Sports Hall of Fame secured some federal funds in 1970, and at present has some well-qualified personnel engaged in a project to collate material pertaining to Canada's rich heritage in sport.

The Hockey Hall of Fame building is comprised of three main levels: (a) a main exhibition hall at ground level, together with entrance, office, and control rooms, (b) a mezzanine level with a gallery overlooking the main hall, a theater that can accommodate 100 persons, and a library for hockey source material, (c) a basement area, including the main mechanical room, storage rooms and areas, and workshop. The main hall is approximately 130 feet long, 50 feet wide and 18 feet high. Until 1967, it displayed items pertaining to hockey and other sports, but since the addition of a new wing for Canada's Sports Hall of Fame, it is now devoted entirely to hockey. The Hockey Hall of Fame is also the repository for the game's outstanding trophies, including the most famous Stanley Cup. This is exhibited during most of the year except when removed for official presentation, alterations, or repairs. More than 125 of hockey's renowned past players have been elected to the hall, as well as more than 40 "builders" of the game, and 7 referees.

The Hockey Hall of Fame book, *Hockey's Heritage,* which contains pictures and profiles of each honored member's career, is available from the hall, price $2.50. It was prepared and edited by the active curator of both institutions, Mr. M. H. ("Lefty") Reid. The building is open daily, except Christmas and New Year's Day, from 2 P.M. to 4 P.M. (Additional hours can be reserved for special functions). During the Canadian National Exhibition, from late August to early September, it is open from 9 A.M. to 10 P.M. Special arrangements can be made for visiting groups, including the showing of hockey films.

THE K. A. AUTY MEMORIAL LIBRARY, RIDLEY COLLEGE, ST. CATHERINES

Ontario

One of the world's major collections of cricket literature exists at Ridley College in St. Catherines, Ontario. This is the K. A. Auty Memorial Library, which possesses some 2300 volumes, as well as miscellaneous booklets, pamphlets, papers, and photographs.

Karl Auty made a lifetime hobby of collecting cricket literature. He searched far and wide, making hundreds of friends in the process and writing thousands of letters. His apartment was actually a cricket library, complete with an index file and cross-reference system. He was president of the Chicago Cricket Club and the Illinois Cricket Association for many years, an active cricketer until his late sixties, and he particularly enjoyed his games at Ridley College.

After Mr. Auty's death in 1959, his cricket collection was bequeathed to Ridley College. A cricketing colleague, Harry Gawthorp, made a generous endowment to the college to ensure the maintenance of the library, and other additions have since been made by purchase and donation. The librarians are always glad to hear from anyone interested in this unique collection, or from persons who might be willing to contribute new material.

Canada

THE NATIONAL SKI MUSEUM
457A Sussex Drive, Ottawa, Ontario

The National Ski Museum is now located in larger quarters on the second floor of 457A Sussex Drive, on the Mile of History, in the capital city of Ottawa. The concept was first given recognition by the Canadian Ski Association during Canada's Centennial Year, and the official opening of the National Ski Museum in May, 1971, marked the 50th anniversary of the association.

The theme of the museum is: "Skiing in its meaningful context in the development of Man." Its *raison d'être* was given by Mr. Rae Grinnell, Chairman of the Museum Committee: "From man's earliest beginnings, one dimension of freedom has been mobility. The elements, particularly snow, contrived against him; movement and survival were synonymous. Two thousand or more years ago, need and ingenuity created the first primitive ski. They served both hunter and the hunted. Out of their ability to provide flight over deep snow came pleasure and communication. A new sport was born. Remote winter villages emerged from their isolation. Technology and competition advanced the sport to new levels of delight. To the young at heart, skiing has become a way of life."

The skiing way of life has naturally a rich tradition in Canada which the National Ski Museum aims to preserve. As early as 1879, a Mr. A. Birch of Montreal skied 170 miles to Quebec City using 9-ft. skis and a single pole. In 1887, Lord Frederick Hamilton, then A.D.C. to the Governor-General, introduced the sport to Ottawa by skiing at Rockcliffe Park, to the derision of his friends. Ski-jumping was recorded at Revelstoke, B.C., in 1890, and seven years later Olaus Jeldness won the first downhill race on Red Mountain, Rossland, B.C.

The Museum Committee members have collected artifacts pertaining to this heritage as well as compiling a written and pictorial record. The exhibits date back nearly a century to the early rudimentary equipment, but there are also recent medals and racing equipment from international ski competitions. At the time of publication the opening hours for the National Ski Museum had not been finally determined. There is not expected to be any admission charge.

THE CANADIAN FOOTBALL HALL OF FAME, CIVIC CENTER, adjacent CITY HALL

Hamilton, Ontario

The first steps towards the establishment of a hall of fame in which the rich heritage of Canadian Football could be recognized and preserved occurred in 1961. In the following year, the mayor of Hamilton on behalf of the city, offered a site for such an institution. This was accepted, a Selection Committee and directors were appointed, and the first charter members—in the two categories of "builders" and "players"—were elected in 1963. Other members were elected in succeeding years, and on March 12, 1970, the first sod was turned for the Canadian Football Hall of Fame building in Hamilton.

Construction of the $400,000 two-story building has now been completed, and the interior will be equipped at an estimated cost of a further $300,000. The Canadian Football Hall of Fame was opened in 1972, probably "the first electronic sports history center of this kind." Modern technology is being employed to present the story of Canadian football in a unique manner. The first computer record book will enable visitors to have their questions answered by the football computer from its input of the Canadian Football League Record Book. The history of the league and various teams will be presented on monitors, in color, with audio-commentary available at the push of a button. The Grey Cup Section of the exhibit area will reproduce the excitement of Canada's biggest sports event in sound and film, and the Hall of Fame Theater will also utilize latest equipment. The museum section will feature steel-sculptured busts of the players and builders of Canadian football, an illuminated summary of each career, and recordings of their voices.

The Canadian Football Hall of Fame is well situated in a central location near the City Hall, Educational Center, Public Library, and Art Gallery; its innovative exhibitions will no doubt be enjoyed by many visitors to Hamilton in the years to come.

Canada

DATES: All year round. Closed Christmas Day, New Year's Day and Easter Sunday.
HOURS: 9:30 A.M. to 4:30 P.M. every day.
ADMISSION: Adults $1.00–$.50 under 14–$2.00 family group
Special admission rates for groups of more than 10–half price.

DAREDEVIL HALL OF FAME

(Located in the Niagara Falls Museum)
Niagara Falls, Canada

The Daredevil Hall of Fame is only one of twenty-six galleries in the Niagara Falls Museum, but the displays of equipment used by those who survived the plunge over the Falls and the authentic tableaux depicting the death-defying feats have made it a feature attraction. Founded in 1827 for the purpose of making available for public viewing a zoological exhibit and a collection of valuable and rare specimens of natural history, the museum has been expanded to include some of the finest collections and specimens to be found anywhere in the world.

Daredevils have performed on tightwires above the gorge, beginning with the Great Blondin in 1859, drowned while attempting to swim Whirlpool Rapids, as did Captain Matthew Webb, the first person to swim the English Channel, shot the Upper, Lower, and Whirlpool Rapids in different flotation devices with varying success, and made the run over Horseshoe Falls in wooden barrels, rubber balls and inflated tubes. The first to conquer Horseshoe Falls was Anna Taylor, a school teacher, who made the trip in 1901. Sixty years later, six men had attempted to duplicate her feat and only three survived the ordeal.

Events in which challengers were successful have been authentically and realistically created through the effective use of dioramas and displays of equipment in the Daredevil Hall of Fame. Whether the visitor stands before the artists' conception of that dramatic moment when bruised and battered Anna Taylor emerged from her now-historic barrel to hear "Good God, she's alive!," or the rubber ball that Jean Lussier used in 1928, the past pushes aside the present.

Housed in the other twenty-five galleries are an array of interesting and informative collections. The extensive Egyptian Collection includes a magnificently preserved mummy which dates from 1530 B.C., and the collection of fossil species, located in the Hall of Dinosaurs Exhibit, contains items which record 540 million years of history.

Canada

Among the other collections are ancient arms and weaponry, Oriental curios, Indian lore, wildlife, and minerals.

DATES: Daily
HOURS: Summer—8:30 A.M. to 12 midnight
Winter—9:30 A.M. to 6 P.M.
ADMISSION: Adults $1.50
Students under 16 $.75—Children 6 and under—FREE
Special group rates are available upon written request.

AQUATIC HALL OF FAME AND MUSEUM OF CANADA INC.

Pan-Am Pool, 25 Poseidon Bay, Winnipeg, Manitoba

The City of Winnipeg is the sponsor of the Aquatic Hall of Fame and Museum of Canada Inc., which was established in 1967, during the centennial of the Province of Manitoba. The Pan-Am Pool complex was built at a cost of more than $3 million, on more than 13 acres of land. At the pool's inauguration, water was brought from the Atlantic, the Pacific, and the Arctic Oceans for the ceremony. Being located at Poseidon Bay, named after the Greek god of the sea and protector of all waters, water was also brought from Greece for the dedication of the street. The three levels of government, i.e. federal, provincial, and city, were all represented on this special occasion.

The Aquatic Hall of Fame and Museum of Canada Inc. pays tribute to those in swimming, diving, water polo, and synchronized swimming, who have attained international renown, or given distinguished service to these sports. A committee of the Ladies of the Aquatic Hall of Fame and Museum is most active and assists in the various events at the natatorium. More than $150,000 worth of items have already been donated. The oldest Cutty Sark Club in the world was formed in Winnipeg in 1932, and the members have donated all their ship models and memorabilia to the Aquatic Hall of Fame and Museum. One of the models is valued at over $10,000. The club now has its headquarters in "The Suite" at the Pan-Am Pool. As well as this fine meeting place, there is also an ample research center and library, plus films, together with a large boardroom for meetings.

The ancient history of aquatics is particularly well depicted at this excellent institution. The Aquatic Hall of Fame and Museum of Canada Inc. has on display the only copies in the world of exquisite artifacts, such as the bronze statuette of a diver attributed to about 460 B.C., found in Perugia, Italy, the original of which is in the Museum of Antique Arts, Munich, Germany. Also featured is a copy of the famous relief located in the British Museum, London, dating back to 880 B.C. and taken from the Palace of Nimroud, which depicts fugitives escaping from soldiers by swimming a river, one using the over-arm crawl stroke, and others using under-water air skins. There is in addition a large photograph of a painting recently discovered among tombs near the Temple of Neptune in Paestum, south of Naples, Italy. It shows a young ephebe, poised between sky and sea, executing a high dive. The discovery was named "Tomba del Tuffatore" ("The Tomb of the Diver") and dated from 480 B.C.

Vaughan Lawson Baird, Q.C., has been chairman since the inception of the Aquatic Hall of Fame and Museum Inc. at Winnipeg. Visitors to the city are well advised to view this magnificent facility and assured of a most rewarding experience. It is open every day from 9 A.M. till 10 P.M. throughout the year. Admission is free.

AQUARIUM AND HORSEMAN'S HALL OF FAME

1892 15th Street S.E., Calgary 22, Alberta

In the beautiful gardens of the Calgary Brewing and Malting Company Limited is one of the most unique halls of fame in North America, situated in the upper floor of the Aquarium building. This company sponsors and maintains the famous Aquarium and Horseman's Hall of Fame, two attractions that combine to attract over 200,000 visitors annually.

Both were established by the Calgary Brewing and Malting Company Limited as a salute to the men and women who built the West for future generations. The Horseman's Hall of Fame, opened in 1963, features dioramas, shadow boxes, life-size models, early guns, sculptures, ceramic portraits, and many artifacts, all expertly displayed in extremely attractive surroundings. The "Men of our Day" exhibit is a tribute to men who have helped to shape the destiny of the West. One scene depicts the beginning of the world-famous Calgary Stampede in 1912. Another re-enacts the historic signing of Blackfoot Treaty Number Seven, which assured peace between Indians and settlers in western Canada. The interesting gun collection includes a pistol owned by Louis Riel. Chuckwagon drivers, rodeo riders, cowboy-artist Charles Russell, and other famous individuals of the West, are all honored by informative displays. There are also extensive Indian crafts and horseman exhibits, a Red River Cart, and a large historical map of Alberta. Among the unique features is a "Brand Ceiling" that shows early Alberta horse brands that are still registered and in use today.

The Aquarium was built in 1960, when the seawater was brought by truck from Vancouver, B.C. Being Canada's only inland aquarium, it is replaced by this method every two years, while a complex filtration system keeps the water clear and fresh in the interval. Approximately 100,000 gallons of salt and fresh water are kept in constant circulation. The tanks are divided into 5 separate systems: tropical freshwater 75° F., temperate freshwater 65° F., cold freshwater 50° F., tropical seawater 75° F., cold seawater 50° F. More than 1000 specimens from all over the world can be seen in about 60 exhibits. These include an alligator from Florida, sea horses from the Caribbean, man-eating piranhas from the Amazon River of South America, the native aholehole fish from Hawaii, an electric eel, nurse sharks, lake sturgeons, giant green sea turtles, and even an "up-side-down catfish" found only in Africa. Many more fish, reptiles, invertebrates, and amphibians can be viewed in this remarkable facility.

Without doubt, any visitor to western Canada will be well rewarded by a visit to the beautiful Calgary Brewery Gardens and its Aquarium and Horseman's Hall of Fame. The curator is Mr. K. N. Zurosky, and it is open from 10 A.M. to 5 P.M. every day, except Christmas Day and New Years Day.

ADMISSION: Adults (18 years and over), $.50 each
Children (6 to 17 years inclusive), $.25 each
Senior citizens, FREE
Children's educational groups, FREE
Adult groups, tours, etc., $.40 each

THE EDMONTON HALL OF FAME, EDMONTON GARDENS

118 Avenue and 75 Street, Edmonton, Alberta

The Edmonton Hall of Fame was first structured in 1961, and its purpose is to honor outstanding city athletes or persons who have rendered prolonged and meritorious service to sports activities in the City of Edmonton. Amateur or professional member athletes must have retired from active competition, and usually have been resident in Edmonton for at least ten consecutive years. The same residential qualification applies to other members, who also must have served sport for at least ten years, not necessarily consecutive, on a voluntary basis.

The hall of fame is situated at the entrance to the Edmonton Gardens. A leather-bound register outlines the achievements of each of the members of the hall of fame and catalogs them numerically. These numbers correspond with photographs of the members, which are displayed in four large glass show cases. Among the most recent members are Jesse Jones, a noted amateur track and field athlete, Frank Morris, who had a long and distinguished career in Canadian Football, and Patricia Underhill, the Canadian Women's Outdoor Speed Skating Champion and Coach, who was awarded a Centennial medal in 1967 for outstanding service to her country.

The Edmonton Gardens are open to the public during normal business hours and there is no admission charge for the hall of fame. Admission to the many sporting events that take place in the Gardens, i.e. hockey games, Edmonton's famous "Klondike Days," etc., also allows spectators to view the hall of fame at their leisure.

THE BRITISH COLUMBIA SPORTS HALL OF FAME, B.C. PAVILION, PACIFIC NATIONAL EXHIBITION

Exhibition Park, Vancouver 6

The British Columbia Sports Hall of Fame is registered as a Public Non-Profit Society, and was mainly established by a grant from the British Columbia Centennial Committee. It was formally opened in 1966, and is situated in the B.C. Pavilion on the grounds of the Pacific National Exhibition. Since then, it has established a policy of self-support through a select program of special events. The Sports Hall of Fame is a permanent tribute to the achievements of the province's outstanding athletes, administrators, builders, and coaches.

Inside the hall, the history of many sports is traced through the displays of artifacts, mementos, photographs, and scrapbooks. Included in this memorabilia is a notable collection of Olympic, Pan-American, and Commonwealth Games medals. Those athletes elected to the British Columbia Sports Hall of Fame are featured in their appropriate sport sections. They must have demonstrated their capability at national or international level, or performed in a manner which brought special honor to the province. An equally high standard of admission is required of the administrators and builders elected, also. To date, 66 individuals and 2 rowing crews have been elected, including Mary Stewart and Elaine Tanner (swimming), Percy Williams and Harry Jerome (sprinting), Jimmy McLarnin (boxing), Nancy Greene Raine (skiing), and Doug Hepburn (weightlifting).

HOURS: 10 A.M. to 5 P.M. weekdays
1 P.M. to 5 P.M. Sunday
ADMISSION: FREE

THE BRITISH COLUMBIA SKI HALL OF FAME, ROSSLAND HISTORICAL MUSEUM

Junctions of Highways 22 and 3B, Rossland, British Columbia

The Rossland Historical Museum was officially opened on July 4, 1967, in a building that had been constructed for use as a museum and tourist information center by the Rossland Canadian Confederation Centennial Committee as part of the centennial complex. Rossland is the western gateway to the Kootenays, and because of its rich gold mines was early dubbed "The Golden City." A business area on Columbia Avenue in the town is 3410 feet above sea level. In recent years, however, Rossland has acquired new fame through the sport of skiing.

The Nancy Greene Wing was built onto the Rossland Historical Museum with the help of a British Columbia Government grant to honor her achievements in her home town. The Provincial Government has designated it as the official British Columbia Ski Hall of Fame. It was officially opened by Nancy Greene Raine in May, 1970.

The displays include Nancy Greene's two World Cups, Olympic medals, F.I.S. medals, and many other trophies from her brilliant career. Items of her championship ski equipment are also displayed, as well as her first "good" pair of skis. A colorful collection of her winning tie-on race numbers, and international flags used at the du Maurier World Cup races held at Rossland in 1968, are also featured.

There is also an Olaus Jeldness display that includes his ten-foot skis, medals, and trophies. The centerpiece of this display is the large ornate silver cup donated by Jeldness himself for future competition. It was Jeldness who introduced skiing to Rossland in 1896, and who became the first Dominion champion in both ski "running" and jumping four years later. His favorite hill was Red Mountain, which is the home hill of Nancy Greene and the renowned Red Mountain Ski Club.

Adequate parking is provided and there are picnic tables on the site. No visit to this quiet residential town, only 5 air miles north of the International Border, would be complete without taking the opportunity to enjoy the variety of exhibits offered in its unique historical museum.

DATES: Mid-May until mid-September daily
By appointment off season
ADMISSION: $.35

The Canadian Golf Museum. (Courtesy Canadian Golf Museum)

Historical Stone Clubhouse (1812), home of the Canadian Golf Museum, Kingsway Park, Quebec. (Courtesy Canadian Golf Museum)

The International Hockey Hall of Fame. (Courtesy International Hockey Hall of Fame)

174　　　　　　　　　　　　　　　　　　　　　　　　SPORTING HERITAGE

An exhibit at the International Hockey Hall of Fame. (Courtesy International Hockey Hall of Fame)

Canada's Sports Hall of Fame, and Hockey Hall of Fame, Exhibition Park, Toronto 2B, Canada. (Courtesy Canada's Sports Hall of Fame and Hockey Hall of Fame)

The Stanley Cup, Hockey Hall of Fame, Toronto. (Courtesy Canada's Sports Hall of Fame and Hockey Hall of Fame)

Official Opening—Hockey Hall of Fame—August 26, 1961. (Courtesy Canada's Sports Hall of Fame and Hockey Hall of Fame)

Sawchuk and goalie display—1971–72. (Courtesy Canada's Sports Hall of Fame and Hockey Hall of Fame)

Canada 177

Gordie Howe pix board. (Courtesy Canada's Sports Hall of Fame and Hockey Hall of Fame)

Six-ft. ski with leather-covered cane binding used in Ottawa in the early 1900s by Frank Bedard, a founding member of the Ottawa Ski Club. (Courtesy Morley Roberts)

Canada

The opening ceremonies at the museum. (Courtesy National Ski Museum)

H. Smith Johannsen, still skiing at age 97. He laid out the famous Maple Leaf Trail in the Laurentians and has been instrumental in determining the locations of many eastern Ontario ski areas. (Courtesy National Ski Museum)

The Canadian Football Hall of Fame, Hamilton, Ontario. (Courtesy Hamilton Fire Dept.)

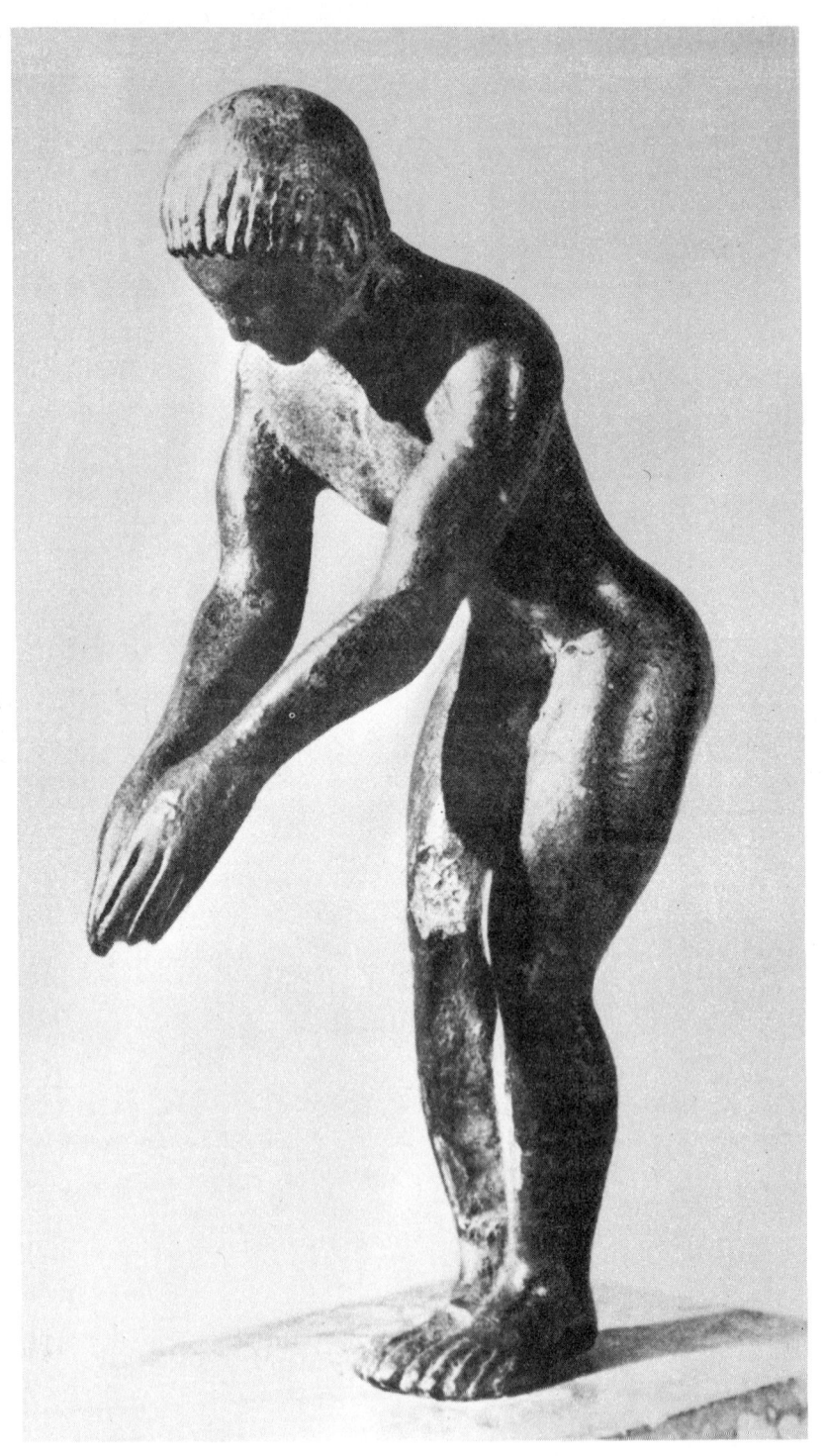

The Aquatic Hall of Fame and Museum of Canada has the only copy in the world of a bronze statuette of a diver, attributed to about 460 B.C., found in Perugia, Italy. The original is in the Museum of Antique Arts, Munich, Germany. (Courtesy The Aquatic Hall of Fame and Museum of Canada)

Calgary Horseman's Hall of Fame, Calgary, Alberta, Canada. (Courtesy Calgary Horseman's Hall of Fame)

Display cases at the British Columbia Sports Hall of Fame, Vancouver, Canada. (Courtesy British Columbia Sports Hall of Fame)

The International Honour Roll, where all B.C. athletes who won gold, silver, or bronze medals in international games, are listed. The listing goes as far back as the 1912 Olympics. (Courtesy British Columbia Sports Hall of Fame)

The Nancy Greene Wing of the Rossland Museum, B.C. Ski Hall of Fame—part of its display. The spectators are R.K.W. (Bob) Greene, Mrs. (Helen) Greene, and Ricky Greene. (Courtesy British Columbia Ski Hall of Fame)

The Nancy Greene Wing of the Rossland Museum, B.C. Ski Hall of Fame—a close-up of a display. (Courtesy British Columbia Ski Hall of Fame)

The Nancy Greene Wing of the Rossland Museum—Jeldness display. (Courtesy British Columbia Ski Hall of Fame)